THE SLAVE

Geoffrey Fielden

Bloomington, IN

authorHOUSE®

Milton Keynes, UK

AuthorHouse™
1663 Liberty Drive, Suite 200
Bloomington, IN 47403
www.authorhouse.com
Phone: 1-800-839-8640

AuthorHouse™ UK Ltd.
500 Avebury Boulevard
Central Milton Keynes, MK9 2BE
www.authorhouse.co.uk
Phone: 08001974150

First published by AuthorHouse 8/7/2007

ISBN: 978-1-4259-6614-0 (sc)

Printed in the United States of America
Bloomington, Indiana
This book is printed on acid-free paper.

Special thanks to my very good friend David Temlett whose insight helped clarify many of the ideas expressed in this book.

~ Foreword ~

I am not a politically correct person. Nor will I ever be. I have no feeling of guilt in this regard whatsoever and I will apologise to no one for it. I do not call mankind, humankind, I do not call students, learners and I do not call manpower, peoplepower. As far as I am concerned, words such as chairman are not, and never were, intended to be gender specific. I use the word "he" to denote both male and female gender. Those who don't like it need read no further.

I believe that such causes as woman's rights, gay rights, lesbian rights, black rights, old people's rights, the unborn's rights and such like, are irrational red herrings. In my opinion, all individuals should have exactly the same rights, and that's what they should properly be called – **individual rights**, not human rights or any other type of rights.

I use reason and logic, not emotions and feelings to form my opinions and beliefs; in other words, my philosophy is objective.

I believe in the individual; that Man's ego is of paramount importance. I deplore tribalism, collectivism (including all forms of statism) and any form of mysticism. They are cancerous diseases all.

It is my sincere opinion that unless a rational code of morality is developed and adopted, the world, and the Western world in particular, is on the brink of a disaster, the like of which has not been seen since the Dark Ages; the scale of which has never before been experienced. Many books have been written over the last two hundred years or so on this and similar subjects. For all intents and purposes they have been ignored. I don't expect any better reception to this book. But those who do choose to read it will no longer be able to claim they weren't warned or didn't know; and at least I will have tried.

~ PROLOGUE ~

In spite of the ferocious display of lightning that lit up the night sky and the deafening, almost frightening sound of thunder, the throng of passengers left the shelter of the terminal that used to be known as Jan Smuts International but had since been renamed Johannesburg International Airport and boarded the British Airways Boeing 747. When the standard safety preliminaries were completed, the gigantic plane taxied down the runway flinging a jet of spray behind it, almost in contempt of the storm overhead. It gathered speed rapidly, its wheels left the tarmac and it rose steadily into the night sky. James Bradshaw peered through the window and watched the lights of Johannesburg gradually grow smaller and smaller. The plane forced its way through the clouds, banked to starboard and as the lights disappeared from view he saw only darkness. How fitting, he thought, as he said goodbye to Africa. He settled his lean frame into his non-too comfortable economy class seat, pushed his brown wavy hair back from his forehead with his fingers. As the plane reached its optimum altitude and was levelling off, an attractive stewardess approached with a drinks trolley and Bradshaw ordered a whisky. She handed him the drink and he sipped it slowly. The non-stop flight to Heathrow would take about eleven hours and he settled back for the long flight. Normally not one to dwell on the past, it however seemed appropriate to reflect on the last twenty odd years of his life. He took another sip of whisky, closed his eyes and let the events of the last two decades flow like a motion picture through his mind.

He pictured himself arriving in South Africa from England in 1979 as a disenchanted 31 year old and had lived there ever since. He chuckled quietly to himself. In hindsight, this was the time for anyone in his right mind to be making plans to leave the country. Regardless of the problems that had existed at the time, largely as a result of the cruel policy of Apartheid, the subsequent changes which resulted from democratic elections and a new dispensation, the country had steadily gone downhill ever since. Hindsight was indeed a marvellous thing. But at the end of the seventies, England had suffered for far too long under the immoral and disastrous experiment with Socialism, perpetuated by successive Labour governments and not reversed to any significant degree by the Conservatives when they were in office. Just what it was the Conservative Party was trying to conserve had eluded him. If it wasn't the free market system and the protection of the rights of the individual and his property, then what else could it be? Years of oppressive government, persecution instead of incentives for personal achievement and success, draconian taxation and a general atmosphere of despair, exacerbated by hooligan trade union action hell bent on anarchy and the destruction of the British economy, had driven Bradshaw and tens of thousands like him to try greener pastures in the far flung corners of what used to be the Empire. Anyone with any get-up-and-go had got up and gone. Someone by the name of Margaret Thatcher had just been elected Prime Minister and she had promised, during her campaign, serious reforms if elected, but James Bradshaw had heard it all before, had had enough and had set off to Africa.

He had worked for several different companies during the subsequent years and had always taken his jobs seriously and because of his hard work and the results he had achieved, he had always been well thought of and had been rewarded with modest promotion. The only obstacle to greater success had been his abhorrence of the corporate environment where sycophancy not only flourished, but was compulsory. The higher one climbed the corporate ladder, the more one was required to be a yes-man. He could not bring himself to laugh at the inane jokes told by his superiors, or socialise with his bosses in order to gain further rewards. When asked for his opinion he had given it in an open and honest manner. To his cost, he realised too late, that it was not his opinion his employers wanted, but his agreement, his concurrence, his compliance; his agreement with any and every idea they had thought of, whether it had any merit or not. In the corporate world, honesty was definitely not the best policy. Hence his career proceeded down the road of mediocrity instead of reaching the extent of his ability. More than once he had been told he was not a company man, that he had a problem with his attitude and he was perceived as negative, and once, to clear out his desk as his services were no longer required. A wry smile crossed his face as he took another sip of scotch. C'est la vie.

Changing tack, he reflected on his romances with a mixture of affection and disappointment. For better or worse he had never married, though he had been close on one or two occasions. Socially, he had made plenty of acquaintances, a few of which had developed into good friends, but for the most part he had preferred his own company for he did not suffer fools lightly. Most of his friends were of a similar age to himself, intelligent and he had enjoyed the good times they shared. Sadly, one had been killed in a senseless and cowardly bomb attack by the ANC on a restaurant during the political violence that had plagued the eighties and early nineties.

And then there had been the new ANC government with its dubious record. And a new constitution. And a new dispensation. Several of his friends had been forced into premature unemployment as a result of the new government's racial policy of affirmative action, and had fallen on hard times resulting in an almost inescapable poverty. Far too many of the evils of the Apartheid years were being perpetuated in a different form under the new regime. For Bradshaw, the most disgusting aspect of this new form of racism was that it was instigated, promoted and somehow justified by the very people who claimed to have fought for equality and freedom. It was hypocrisy in its most blatant form. Black oppressors had merely replaced white oppressors. Apart from a new black elite, mostly benefactors of nepotism, the average black South African was no better off than under the Apartheid regime and in many cases was worse off. Nonetheless they had their freedom, or so they thought.

And then there had been the new taxes, which were designed to "more fairly" redistribute the nation's wealth. Bradshaw had argued that a nation per se has no wealth. Only individuals living in that nation can create and possess wealth, and the only fair and just way of distributing it is by the ability of each individual to earn it. There can be no way to "more fairly redistribute" another's property and any attempt to do so is a form of legalised theft – which in fact, all taxes are.

Bradshaw's retirement plan had been to own three or four houses and to rent them out, thus providing a comfortable income in his old age. Then there had been the piece of legislation that defied all logic; defaulters of mortgage or rent payments could no longer be evicted except after an expensive, drawn-out process that included court orders. Many feared that the government was following the path of that madman to the north – Mugabe. Some were outraged and complained but few would listen and even fewer would act, so these taxes, that in effect penalised only the white community, increased in number and severity and conversely services they were designed to pay for decreased in number and effectiveness. There had been mass resignations from the police force; government run hospitals became little more than stepping-stones to the afterlife and schooling deteriorated to levels never before experienced in the country's history. And then there had been Dave O'Brian, originally from Dublin and one of Bradshaw's closest friends, who, due to the appalling condition of the government run hospitals, and the even more appalling level of expertise, was forced to sell his house in order to pay for an unsuccessful operation in a private hospital. Totally disillusioned, O'Brian had returned to Ireland, only to die a short time later. Crime was endemic. Minimal sentences were often handed out to hardened, violent criminals. The streets weren't safe for man or beast. The exchange rate had slipped to all time lows against the major currencies and inflation was once again in double digits. Unemployment was hovering above forty percent. So much for the New South Africa. But most offensive of all to Bradshaw, was the way that the vast majority of whites divorced themselves from reality and lived in a comatose state, believing that all was well and desperately reinforcing this belief by monotonously repeating mindless mantras to such a degree that most Tibetan priests would have been exhausted.

Regardless of one's perspective, the truth was that Africa was no more a place for a white male over the age of forty, let alone approaching fifty. Men in this category, the currently disadvantaged, had replaced the previously disadvantaged, and nobody gave a damn. So with a great deal of regret and apprehension, Bradshaw had decided to leave Africa for good and return to the country of his birth. Deciding that he must first obtain a qualification that would be recognised internationally, at the age of forty-nine he had resigned from his job and enrolled in a full time computer course. After five months of blood, sweat and tears and shortly after his fiftieth birthday, he had passed his final exam and received his qualification as a network systems engineer.

Finding employment in the world of IT had proved quite easy; the Y2K panic was at its height and qualified computer people were in demand despite their having little or no experience and Bradshaw was soon part of a team contracted by a major bank to ensure its computers were Y2K compliant. The downside was that he had to work for a salary far less than he was used to earning, as many youngsters less than half his age, were competing in the market place and were prepared to work for minimal salaries. Bradshaw didn't object to this; he believed in the free market system of supply and demand, and even though it would put severe financial constraints upon him, at least he was earning some money and more importantly gaining valuable experience in the world of computers. Well, that's what he had thought. The Y2K work usually entailed loading software and service patches on countless computers each day. The work was routine and boring. He was gaining experience, but it was the same experience every day. Instead of gaining a year's experience after twelve months, at this rate he would have one day's experience multiplied by three hundred and sixty five. This was certainly not going to enhance his curriculum vitae or his future.

With the Y2K scare finally over, Bradshaw's contract had ended and so had his prospects of earning a viable living in South Africa. But he had gained some experience, so he had sold his house, his furniture and car, said his farewells and boarded the plane in which he now sat. In spite of the boast of the new government that South Africa had "the best constitution in the world", he was still not permitted by law to transfer all of his money to England. So much for property rights. This would have to be done over a period of time, though with the exchange rate at fifteen to one against him, this did not have the impact it normally would. Nonetheless, his standard of living back in England would be substantially reduced until he re-established himself, but he believed that the long-term prospects would be far better.

The pilot's voice interrupted his thoughts. Or was it his sleep? The plane was about to make its final approach. Bradshaw rubbed his eyes, put on his seat belt as the pilot's voice had requested and looked out of the window. Still far below he could make out the English Channel in the morning sun and the numerous ships that crossed it, bring trade from across the globe. The sky was clear but as the plane approached the coastline it was met by a bank of whitish grey cloud that, except for a few open patches, blanketed his view of the mainland. It was as though a huge cloud, the precise size and shape of England hovered over it. He had noticed this on previous flights and wondered if it was the same cloud; whether it was a permanent fixture.

The plane landed without event and Bradshaw passed quickly through immigration and then customs. He was impressed with the efficiency. Then again, an airport the size of Heathrow had to be efficient just to survive. He made his way to the Underground and caught the tube via the Piccadilly Line to Hounslow West. He had chosen to initially base himself in the Hounslow area, not only because it was situated on the Underground route, but of its proximity to London and also because accommodation would be cheaper, though not much, than in London itself. The Underground at Hounslow West is not actually under the ground, but above ground like a conventional train. As he emerged from the relative warmth of the train, the cold, damp February wind bit sharply. The change from the summer heat of Africa was dramatic. Fortunately Bradshaw had put on gloves and wrapped a scarf around his neck before boarding the tube. He found the station porter and asked if he could leave his luggage at the station for a few hours. The porter told him abruptly that it wasn't normal practice, but he became much more friendly and co-operative after Bradshaw had pushed a five-pound note into his hand. Free of encumbrances, he set off on foot in search of accommodation. The main street was only a short distance from the station and Bradshaw rubbed his hands together to keep them warm as he strode quickly from the station, over the old stone railway bridge and into the town. There were several estate agencies to choose from, all with pictures of properties for sale displayed in their front windows. He looked the asking prices of some of the more modest homes and felt quite nauseous. The exchange rate was going to kill him. He found an estate agency that had "Property to Rent" listed in one of its side windows and went inside. He was greeted by a pleasant looking woman who referred him to a bespectacled man in a tweed jacket. Bradshaw explained that he was looking for something to rent; something not too expensive.

'Is it just for yourself, sir?' asked the man in the tweed jacket.

Yes.' replied Bradshaw, 'Just myself.' Periodically Bradshaw heard a 'Hum' or 'Ah' as Mr Tweed-Jacket flipped through his files, stopping every now and again. Finally he glanced up with a look of despondency on his face.

'Not much available.' he said without enthusiasm, 'in fact we've only got one that might suite you I'm afraid. It's a one bedroom flat above a row of shops.' He stared at Bradshaw hopefully.

'I'd like to look at it.' said Bradshaw.

'It's just around the corner.' answered Mr Tweed-Jacket, putting on a heavy topcoat and a pair of leather gloves. 'It will only take a couple of minutes to walk there.' Thankfully the wind had dropped and there was no immediate sign of rain. Bradshaw followed Mr Tweed-Jacket and shortly they rounded a corner and were met by a row of five or six shops. On the corner itself was a general store type of café and next to it a fish and chip shop. Bradshaw also noticed an off-license and something that resembled a bookshop and at the end of the row was a take-away of sorts. The entrance to the upstairs flat lay between the café and the fish and chip shop. Mr Tweed-Jacket produced a key and they climbed the stairs. There was a landing at the top that led to a long narrow passage. Bradshaw counted two doors off to the left and one to the right. They headed for the one on the right and Mr Tweed-Jacket again opened the door. The flat was clean and sparsely furnished but the living area was surprisingly big. A telephone lay on the floor in one corner.

'Does that work?' asked Bradshaw.

'I believe it needs to be re-connected.' replied Mr Tweed-Jacket. Bradshaw went from room to room. Apart from the living area, there was a medium size bedroom, a bathroom that included a shower and a small kitchen. This would do.
'As I said, it's all we have at the moment' said Mr Tweed-Jacket rather apologetically.
I'll take it.' replied Bradshaw.
'Are you sure? We should be getting some more properties in during the next few days. I'm sure we can find something a bit... well a bit more upmarket.'
'I'll take it.' repeated Bradshaw. Mr Tweed-Jacket shrugged his shoulders. They returned to the estate agency where Bradshaw completed the necessary paper work.

He then went to a Barclay's Bank where he cashed some travellers cheques, returned to the estate agency and paid the deposit and first month's rent. Mr Tweed-Jacket shook his hand and Bradshaw went back to the station and collected his bags. He spent the rest of the day settling in. He went out and bought food and other necessities and a street guide from the shops below. He would need to know his way around. Finally he arranged for the phone to be re-connected.

~ Chapter 1 ~

One, two and then three months passed. The cold and rain of winter had given way to spring and the warmer weather that came with it. The café downstairs opened daily at six o'clock to catch the early morning trade and at first Bradshaw had eagerly rushed down the stairs as it opened and bought the newspapers, hurried back upstairs and opened up at the 'Recruitment' section.

There seemed to be ample work in the computer industry and he sent off his CV in response to every position he thought he was sufficiently qualified and experienced to apply for. He was invited to interviews by several companies to discuss the positions with either their IT Managers or the Personnel Departments. He had gone with enthusiasm and returned in frustration for interview after interview had gone un-rewarded. "We'll get back to you Mr Bradshaw." but most of them never did and the few who had the courtesy to contact him always bore bad news. "Thank you for your application Mr Bradshaw, but we've appointed a candidate with more experience." became the standard reply. But Bradshaw soon sensed the real reason for his lack of success; despite his relatively youthful looks, his age was held against him. He had become accustomed to the sly glances and the silly smirks and the disparaging looks on the faces of his interviewers. They seemed to say: "What are you doing applying for a job in computers at your age?" "Don't you know that computers are only for the young?" "If you're older than thirty-five, you're over the hill." "Don't you know that your brain ceased to function years ago?" "Don't waste your time, and more importantly, don't waste ours." "We'll be in touch if we want to see you again." It was not the response he had hoped for.

Late one morning after returning from yet another futile interview, Bradshaw stopped at the grocery shop underneath his flat to buy some bread and milk and found himself the only customer in the shop.
'Still no luck?' enquired old Mr Thomas, the owner. Bradshaw had never mentioned his personal affairs to the old man, but Thomas was no fool. He new Bradshaw bought the newspapers every morning, had watched him board the bus or walk to the Underground station on his way to an interview, dressed in a suite and tie. He had seen Bradshaw return. He had noticed the increasing look of disappointment and frustration on his face.
'Not today.' replied Bradshaw.
'Not that it's any of my business,' continued Thomas, 'but I hear that Paul Crookes is looking for someone. What line of business you in, if you don't mind me askin'?'

Bradshaw smiled to himself. 'Computers.' he replied. 'Or at least I thought so.'
'Don't know nothin' 'bout computers. Mr Crookes he's in the transport business. Got trucks and vans runnin' all over the countryside. Over to France as well.'
'What type of position is he offering?' asked Bradshaw.
'Don't rightly know.' answered Thomas, shaking his head, 'don't think it's computers though.' He hesitated for a moment before he added, 'But it won't do any harm to enquire will it now; better than nothing until something else turns up.' Bradshaw looked at him remaining silent. Thomas interpreted his silence as a cue for him to continue.
'First street passed the station, turn left for about half mile. It's on your left hand side. Can't miss it. There's a big sign saying *Crookes Transport*. You can't miss it.' Bradshaw thanked him, paid for his groceries and went upstairs to his flat. Some post lay on the entrance floor, amongst it a statement from his bank. He opened the envelope and looked at the statement. It was not a pretty sight. And the rent was due again at the end of the week. Bradshaw made himself some lunch and that afternoon he left for Crookes Transport. Old Mr Thomas saw him pass by and smiled to himself.

Crookes Transport was prosperous looking outfit. The double storey office building was modern and the small garden in front was well kept. The large truck and two vans he saw in the parking area appeared well maintained and in good order. Bradshaw entered and was greeted by a young receptionist.

'Good afternoon, I'd like to see Mr Cookes. I was told he has a vacancy.' he said. He was told that Mr Crookes was not available but could Miss Crookes assist? Hopefully she could. The receptionist picked up the phone, looked at Bradshaw and asked.

'Who may I say is calling?'

'James Bradshaw.'

'A Mr Bradshaw, looking for a job.' A short pause. 'Just a moment please.' A few minutes later a slender woman appeared from one of the offices. Suzanne Crookes was in her early forties but wore her years well. Her long raven black hair that matched her equally dark eyes, was drawn back from her forehead and disappeared in a ponytail. She had well defined features and her well-proportioned figure was smartly dressed in a business suite. She had a slight air of indifference about her.

'How may I help you?' she asked eyeing him keenly.

'My name is Bradshaw,' he replied, 'and I was told you have a vacancy.'

'Come into my office.' she said and turned and held her office door open for Bradshaw to enter. She closed the door behind them and motioned him to sit. She went behind her desk and sat down herself. 'My name is Suzanne Crookes. Paul Crookes is my brother. We own this business between us. I run the office, he runs the trucks. And you Mr Bradshaw, what do you do?' Blunt and to the point.

'I'm in computers, but I gather that the position has nothing to do with computers.'

'No. The only position we have is for a van driver's assistant. It pays £5.00 an hour with the opportunity of overtime. You don't look like an assistant Mr Bradshaw.'

'I don't look like a computer person either.' he thought to himself. He took a deep breath. 'I'll take it.' he replied.

'I haven't offered it to you.' She countered. A wry smile crossed his face as Bradshaw looked her in the eyes.

'Well then, I won't waste anymore of your time. Thank you for seeing me Miss Crookes.' And he rose to leave.

'Sit down Mr Bradshaw. The job is yours if you want it. We get a lot of layabouts in here looking for work. A lot of fly-by-nighters and a lot of good-for-nothings, but not many computer people.' she said in the way of explanation.

'I need a job. This is the only one that has been offered to me.'

'At least you're honest, and that makes a change around here. You can start tomorrow morning. Be here at seven thirty sharp Mr Bradshaw.'

~ Chapter 2 ~

'Bradshaw!' Paul Crookes was in his late forties, a tall, large man with a voice to match. He walked towards Bradshaw with a hint of a swagger.

'So you're the new guy.' he said eyeing Bradshaw up and down.

'Yes, James Bradshaw. Miss Crookes said to report here this morning.' Bradshaw extended his right hand.

'You'll be helping Benny. He's over there.' he went on, pointing to a large white Transit van parked about thirty yards away. 'Do as you're told and remember what's in the van is my property, not yours.' He did not shake the offered hand.

'Nice to meet you too.' thought Bradshaw. Instead he replied 'I'll remember that Mr Crookes.' and walked towards the parked van.

'See that you do.' Crookes shouted after him.

Benny Barrett was an overweight, puffy faced individual in his mid thirties and his uncombed greasy hair and missing tooth did nothing to enhance his physical appearance. Neither did his luminous white skin and round shoulders and the size of his stomach would have made a midwife's mouth water. Bradshaw introduced himself and Benny gave him a shifty smile, nodded his head and said, 'So you're my new assistant eh. Just stick with me and I'll show you the ropes. Been doin' this for years. I know all the tricks. Van's all loaded. Get in. We'd better get movin'. Old man Crookes is watchin. Just mind yourself when he's around; he keeps a close eye on all the new guys.' Bradshaw climbed in the passenger's side whilst Benny waddled around to the other side of the van and hauled himself inside. As Benny Barrett started the engine, Bradshaw clipped on his seat belt but noticed that Benny ignored his. Bradshaw didn't enquire whether it was too small or whether Benny was just too lazy to put it on. Benny sniffed and wiped his nose with the back of his sleeve whilst he checked his delivery manifest, shoved the van into gear and wheeled out of the yard and headed towards the motorway.

As they made their deliveries, and when he wasn't sniffing, Benny chatted incessantly.
'What sort of accent is that you've got?'
'South African.' replied Bradshaw.
'How long you been in England?'
'Just over three months.'
'Are you married?'
'No.'

Got any kids?'
'No kids.'
'Me, I'm not married either.' said Benny. 'Can't be bovvered. Still live wiff me muvver. Anyway, who wants to get married wiff all that young single stuff about.' he snorted lewdly. 'Know what I mean?' Bradshaw didn't reply and looked through the side window ignoring him.
'Where d'ya live?' asked Benny, changing the subject.
'I've got a flat not far from Crookes Transport.' replied Bradshaw, not wanting to be any more specific.
'Want to get ya'self a council house.' said Benny, 'Go and see the council. Let the council pay most of the rent and if anything breaks, they've got to fix it. That's what me and me muvver does. I've lived there me whole life. Best thing to do. Why spend me own money when someone else'll pay?'
'Wonderful,' thought Bradshaw, 'just my luck to get stuck with an ambitionless parasite. Never mind, I won't be working here for too long. Something better's got to turn up sooner or later.' In the meantime he'd just have to grin and bare it.

And so Benny's babblings continued, day after day after day. Fortunately Bradshaw soon discovered that if he mouthed an occasional "really" or "is that so" or "you don't say" Benny seemed contented. It was the sound of his own voice that he really enjoyed listening to. Benny had apparently been driving a van for Crookes Transport since he left school and seemed content to achieve no more in life. He had a sister of dubious morals whose sole contribution to mankind thus far was an offering of eight children from six different fathers. And, surprise, surprise, she lived on welfare.

'It's nor fair,' said Benny one day, 'all they'll give 'er's a tiny three bedroom house. Can you imagine the nine of 'em crammed up like that? It's just not fair. She doesn't work. Can't work with all 'em screamin' kids to look after. No wonder she drinks so bleedin' much. It's not 'er fault.'

'And with all the fathers, it must be really overcrowded.' said Bradshaw, not without a hint of sarcasm.

'Doesn't see any of 'em no more. I bump into a couple of 'em in the boozer now and again and the ovvers, I dunno where they are. She's started goin' out with a new fella recently. Just got out of jail. I don't like him. I think she's steppin' down in class.'

'Sounds like it.' replied Bradshaw not trying to conceal his contempt, but Benny seemed not to notice. Most days passed in a similar vane. Benny talking, Bradshaw pretending to listen.

'You know it's not fair,' started Benny yet again, lighting up a cigarette, 'I've been doin' this job now for years and what have I got to show for it? Nothin'. Not a bleedin' thing. Bosses never pay you enough. One day I'm goin' to tell old man Crookes where to stick his job. You just watch me.' He looked at Bradshaw slyly, lowering his voice even though there was no one who could possibly overhear him. 'Don't tell no one, but sometimes I go on unemployment benefits even though I'm still workin'. Got a mate who organises it for me. The bloke the money's supposed to be for died years ago but they don't know about it. There's a few of us what take turns in getting' his benefits. Clever ay? I don't do it all the time mind, jus' when I need extra money. Like when I'm going on holidays or want new clothes or somethin' like that. You know what I mean? I got the right to go on holidays and have decent clothes to wear haven't I?'

A couple of weeks later as they drove out of Crookes yard Benny proudly announced,
'My sister's gettin' a new house real soon. She heard yesterday. Brand new, five bedrooms. Getting' new furniture too. 'Bout bleedin' time. How's she s'pose to bring up all 'em kids in that place she's got now. 'Bout time they gave her somethin' decent.' Bradshaw shook his head in silent disgust. He had come to the conclusion that Benny and his family believed in Heaven – a paradise where all who entered spent each and every day in idle bliss, and consequently they spent their lives on earth practicing for their final destiny. They were bone idle, lazy in the extreme, and had never seen enough reason to make it worth their while to struggle against their natural inclination for mental and physical sloth to achieve a better life for themselves.

Bradshaw and Benny were returning to the yard late one summer's evening when out of the blue Benny asked,
'D'ya want to earn some extra money on he weekend?' Bradshaw was hardly making ends meet on what he was earning. After tax and National Insurance contributions, he was only just managing to pay the bills at the end of each month and that was about all. Despite the small amount of overtime he had been working, there was barely anything left for savings.
'Doing what?' he inquired. Bradshaw didn't trust Benny as far as he could throw him.

'I need a hand to do some deliveries. Know what I mean?' he replied, giving Bradshaw a sly wink.

'No, I don't know what you mean. Why don't you tell me.' Benny became vague, shrugged his shoulders and hummed and haed. 'Spit it out Benny. What are you up to?' Benny was silent for a moment before he went on.

'Don't tell anyone.' he whispered in the conspiratorial tone he used whenever he told Bradshaw about his underhanded dealings. 'This is just between you and me, okay? You know all that stuff we're deliverin' to Morgan's, well I know this bloke who works there – a mate of mine.' In spite of being alone, Benny looked from side to side and lowered his voice even more before continuing. 'Well,' he went on, 'this mate of mine see, he signs in for all the stuff we deliver, but we don't really give him all we're supposed to. He signs that he's received three hundred boxes but we only give him two hundred and fifty. The other fifty you and I take to another mate of mine over in Slough and he gives us thirty quid a box. By the time anyone at Morgan's knows it's missin', they think the stuffs been stolen from their warehouse or somethin' like that. They don't know it's us, see. They'll never suspect we had anythin' to do with it. That's five hundred quid each for a couple of hours work. What d'ya say?

'Forget it Benny. I'm not interested.'

'What's wrong with you? Crookes pays all of us the minimum wage, the tight fisted son of a bitch. Look at that great big Jag he drives around in. And his big fancy house. And as for that snotty nosed sister of his, she ain't got no sense of humour. Thinks she pees eau-de-cologne, she does. It's our hard work that pays for all that. And what do we get? Huh! Peanuts! That's what we get, bleedin' peanuts

'I'm not interested Benny. Count me out.'

'But I need someone to help me unload the stuff at my mates place in Slough.'

"Then ask your mate in Slough to help you.' said Bradshaw.

'He's not goin' to be there and I can't unload the stuff by myself. You know how heavy those boxes are. Come on, no one will ever know. It's money for jam.' Benny persisted. 'Old Crookes is a crook himself. Hey, that's a good joke. Old man Crookes is a crook. Should of thought of that before.' Benny chuckled to himself. 'You know he pays bribes to the local council to do all their deliveries? He doesn't know that I know, but I do. Mate of mine works at the council. He told me. It's worth a fortune that contract. Pays big bribes does Crookes. Why shouldn't we get a piece of the action? Everyone else is.' Bradshaw looked straight in Benny's eyes.

'I told you Benny, I'm not interested. Drop the subject now. If you've got to talk, talk about something else.' They drove back to the yard in silence.

Payday was on each Friday afternoon. The men queued in the reception area at four-thirty in the afternoon and were called one at a time into Suzanne Crookes' office where pay packets were checked and signed for and any discrepancies could be sorted out in private. Suzanne Crookes, as usual was dressed immaculately and her formal manner was extremely businesslike. Benny had described her as "a snotty nosed bitch." "No laughing and joking with her. All work and no play, that's her." When it was Bradshaw's turn, he walked into her office and stood in front of her desk. She looked up and said,

'Mr Bradshaw isn't it?

'Yes Miss Crookes. James Bradshaw.

'Please check your money and sign here for me.' she said, handing him his payslip and an envelope containing a few coins and what seemed to be even fewer notes. Bradshaw checked the cash, signed the slip and passed it back to her.

'It's correct.' he said and turned to leave the office. As he reached the door, her voice asked,

'Are you settling in all right Mr Bradshaw?' The unexpected question caught Bradshaw slightly off guard. He paused for a second.

'Yes thank you Miss Crookes. Everything is fine.'

'Good. Please send in whoever's next.'

Most of the men headed off to the local pub, but Bradshaw declined Benny's insistent pleas for him to join them. Back in his one bedroom flat, Bradshaw counted out his wages and started to prepare his budget. He turned on his laptop computer he had bought with him from South Africa and opened up a spreadsheet he had titled "Monthly Budgets". There were three columns. The first was headed "Expenses", and under which he had listed all his costs and totaled them at the bottom. He entered his income under the second column aptly named "Income", a row for basic wage and a second for overtime. As he pressed the return key, he and glanced across the page and looked under the third column headed "Shortfall/Surplus". Things would be tight. Taxation and National Insurance contributions took too large a slice of his gross wages, but then someone had to foot the bill for Benny's sister and her ilk, and what remained barely covered his expenses. He had budgeted to live off his basic forty-hour weekly wage, which he could just manage to do, but only if he was extremely frugal and incurred no unexpected bills. The only money he was able to save was from overtime whenever it was available, and on that he was taxed at an exorbitant rate. This Chancellor had the conscience of a contract killer and was just as cold blooded. He would never be able to save any sizeable amount of money at this rate. He would never move out of this flat. He would never be able to own his own house, no matter how modest. Even when he managed to get his hands on the rest of his money from South Africa, the exchange rate would ensure it would not make a significant difference. He was going nowhere fast.

In the meantime he continued to look in the newspapers for positions in the computer industry. He phoned for several, but when he mentioned his age, he received the standard reply: "We'll get back to you Mr Bradshaw." None of them ever did. Where to go from here? Definitely not with Benny. Times were tough, but he wasn't a thief. Maybe more overtime. He'd speak to Paul Crookes on Monday.

~ Chapter 3 ~

Monday was a crisp April day and Bradshaw left his flat half an hour earlier than usual. The last traces of the overnight dew were fading as he walked briskly towards Crookes Transport. He found Paul Crookes checking the tyres on one of his larger trucks.

'Morning Mr Crookes.' said Bradshaw. 'May I speak to you for a moment?' Crookes looked up from the tyres and grunted

'What do want Bradshaw? Not a loan I hope. I don't give loans to the staff. If its money you're after, go to a bank.' He carried on inspecting the tyres.

'It is money I'm after Mr Crookes, but I don't want a loan, from either you or the bank.' replied Bradshaw evenly. Paul Crookes looked up sharply. He was used to subservience from his employees; they didn't talk back to him if they knew what was good for them. 'I came to ask you if I could work more overtime.' continued Bradshaw. 'I've been doing some overtime now and then, but I want to do more if it's available.' Crookes stood up to his full height and stared straight at Bradshaw without speaking. Bradshaw stared straight back at him. Finally Paul Crookes said in an almost sneering manner,

'I don't like you or your attitude Bradshaw, but I hear you're honest and work hard. I've got a big contract on the go at the moment and the rest of these lazy bastards won't work an hour longer than they absolutely have to. Can you drive one of these?' he asked, pointing to a three tonner.

'I can drive one.' replied Bradshaw.
'Report to the office at five this afternoon. If it's overtime you want, it's overtime you'll get.' And with that he walked off. Bradshaw arrived at the office at five o'clock sharp and entered by the front door. There was no sign of the receptionist, so he headed towards the door marked "*Paul Crookes*". He was about to knock when he stopped abruptly. There was an awful commotion coming from inside. Paul Crookes' raised voice was bellowing a string of obscenities. Suddenly the door burst open and Suzanne Crookes walked out. When she saw Bradshaw a look of embarrassment came over her and she looked away as she hurried into her own office, closing the door behind her. Paul Crookes charged out of his office.
'Don't you walk away from me when I'm talking to you.' he screamed. Then he saw Bradshaw. 'What the hell do you want?' he bellowed.
'You told me to report here at five o'clock.' replied Bradshaw. 'It's five o'clock.'
'Wait here.' he snapped and barged into his sister's office, slamming the door behind him. After several minutes of rantings and ravings, Paul Crookes emerged. He appeared out of breath and his face was a bluish red colour. He looked at Bradshaw.
'Come with me.' he ordered. Bradshaw followed him outside into the yard. 'Take this truck to Markham and Lewis in Cheltenham. There'll be someone there to help you unload. Here's the address.' He shoved the delivery docket at Bradshaw and stalked off.

For the next few weeks Bradshaw drove to Cheltenham and back every evening from Monday to Thursday. The round trip, including unloading took anywhere from four to four and a half hours, depending on the traffic and it was well after 10 o'clock most nights before he returned to his flat. Each Friday night he turned on his computer and entered the latest figures in his "Monthly Budgets" spreadsheet. The overtime certainly helped in spite of the punitive amount of taxation, and he was able to put a little aside each week into his savings account, but nowhere near enough to make any significant difference to his long-term financial prospects.

Periodically, Benny would gloat about how much he had made on the weekends doing some 'private' work.
'Sure you're not interested?' he would ask now and again.
'How many times do I have to tell you Benny? Count me out!'
'Okay, I'm just askin', that's all.'

The weeks rolled by and turned into months with no prospect of better employment anywhere in sight. The IT market seemed to be getting tighter. After the Y2K scare, there was a glut of computer staff in the market place and accordingly, the years of experience required went up in direct proportion to the amount that salaries went down. Late one evening after returning from Cheltenham and making himself something to eat, Bradshaw turned on his computer to re-examine his financial progress. With all the overtime he was working, he was only managing to save a few pounds but nothing of any real significance. By his best estimation, and with a lot of good fortune, he might be able to afford the deposit on a small flat of his own by the age of fifty-eight. What bank would give a van unloader a mortgage at that age? Even if he managed to get one, it would take twenty years to pay it off. Then allow another ten or fifteen years of saving to put away for his old age. He'd have to work until he was ninety-three years old! The reality was that in all likelihood, he'd have to work until the day he died, with poverty his only companion and that's if anyone would employ him at that age. Bradshaw physically shuddered at the thought. Maybe he could get a job as an antique he thought without humour. His normally positive nature was becoming corrupted with negativity and doubt; an element almost akin to panic began to haunt his very psyche. Something would have to change drastically and very, very soon. Every time he tried to earn more money the taxman stole it from him. He was forced against his will to pay for Benny and his mother, for Benny's sister and her tribe and for thousands of other lazy, dysfunctional parasites who wanted a free ride though life, whilst being deprived of any future for himself. He turned off his computer and walked slowly towards his bedroom. Not even bothering to undress he fell onto his bed and fell into an exhausted sleep.

'Bradshaw,' the icy, toneless voice rang out, 'wake up immediately. What are you doing still sleeping at this hour.' It wasn't a question. 'Get up right now, you should be at work.' Rough invisible hands lifted from his bed shoved him towards the door, down the stairs and out into the street. He stumbled and went sprawling across the footpath. As he looked up, three men dressed in black, with black ski masks and black gloves dragged him to his feet and pushed down the street.

'Keep moving.' barked the voice. Bradshaw rounded the corner and was propelled through some steel gates. Above was a sign, but he couldn't make out what it said. He turned on the three men.
'What the hell's going on?' he yelled. 'Who are you people?'
'Don't asked questions.' snapped the leader of the three men, nodding at the other two. They each responded by grabbing Bradshaw by his arms and shoved him forward towards the rim of a vast opening in the ground. Bradshaw couldn't believe the sight that greeted him. Fifty or sixty feet below was a quarry and hundreds, no thousands of men were labouring. Some were breaking large boulders with sledgehammers, others loading small rail trolleys with shovels. When the trolleys were full they moved off and were replaced by empty ones; just like an endless production line in a factory, it never stopped and no matter how many trolleys were filled, more and more empty ones arrived. All the men were dressed the same in dirty, drab overalls and they all wore a morose, despondent expression.
'Get down there.' ordered the leader of the three men. As mechanically as robots, the two underlings launched Bradshaw over the edge of the abyss. Sheer white-eyed terror gripped him. He was utterly helpless. At first, time seemed to stand still and Bradshaw thought he was floating but the closer he got to the floor of the quarry the faster he fell. He remembered wondering 'Will it hurt when I land?' He also remembered screaming. He awoke violently, drenched in a cold sweat and his heart was pounding, drowning out all other sound. Gradually his breathing slowed, but his hands continued to tremble.

'That was some dream.' he said out aloud in an effort to calm himself. After a long hot shower he dressed for work. 'Another day, another dollar.' he thought and set off to Crookes Transport.

Benny made a habit of stopping at any convenient pub each lunchtime to have a couple of pints of his favourite ale.
'S'all right just to have a couple. No way will I be over the limit. Two doesn't affect me. Been doin' it for years.' he bragged. 'Never been caught.' Bradshaw raised his eyebrows. It was pointless to argue with Benny. He knew it all. And in the afternoons, his prattle became more verbose after the couple that "didn't affect him".
'I'm going to France on the weekend.' he told Bradshaw one afternoon in July. 'Doin' some extra work for the boss. Know what I mean?' He winked slyly. 'Want to come along for the ride?'
'Don't start that again, Benny.
'No, this is legit.' said Benny earnestly. 'Just pickin' up some fags and booze for the boss. It's much cheaper over there. Come along. It won't cost you hardly anything. Old man Crookes pays for the ferry fare for the van, so it's just your fare.'
'Are you sure Benny? There's no funny business?'
'I told you. This is legit. Straight up. Honest.' Actually the idea of a break appealed to Bradshaw, especially after his bad dream. Maybe he was overdoing the overtime. He was tired. He'd been working day and night for weeks and besides, he'd never been to France. Maybe a relaxing weekend would recharge his batteries. Benny was hardly stimulating company but Bradshaw was by now immune to his constant commentary on the unfairness of life.

'Okay Benny, as long as everything's above board I'll go with you.'

Immediately after being paid and clocking out on Friday afternoon Bradshaw and Benny Barrett filled the van with diesel at the company pump and prepared for the drive down to Portsmouth. It would take them between two and two and a half hours. Traffic was a nightmare on Fridays with a lot of people who worked in London during the week returning to the country for the weekend. Fortunately they had plenty of time; the ferry only left at eight that evening. Paul Crookes came towards them.

'You know what to get Benny?' he yelled in his raucous voice. 'Don't mess it up or it'll be the last time you go.'

'I've got it all up here Mr Crookes.' said Benny, tapping his head.

'That's what I'm worried about.' replied Crookes curtly.

'We won't make any mistakes Mr Crookes.' promised Benny.

We, what's this "we" business?'

'Bradshaw's coming with me. Don't worry Mr Crookes,' he added hurriedly, 'he's payin' his own fare.'

'He'd better be.' said Crookes and turned and left them.

~ Chapter 4 ~

The trip to Portsmouth was uneventful. Bradshaw sat back and relaxed and Benny drove. They had just managed to miss the majority of the peak hour traffic and once they turned onto the M3 they cruised along at steady seventy miles per hour.

The summer solstice had occurred a two or three weeks earlier, and that, combined with day light saving, meant that it was still light when they came to a halt at the docks. There were several rows of cars, trucks of varying sizes, vans similar to their own and the like already queuing to pass through customs. Benny came to a halt behind another van and pointed out an office where Bradshaw could buy a ticket. They didn't have to wait long before the vehicles in front of them started to move.

'Let me 'ave your passport.' said Benny as he stopped next to the shed-like building where the customs official sat. Benny handed the passports to him together with the tickets, though the window of the van. The official gave them a perfunctory glance before handing them back and waving them on. The ferry was far larger than Bradshaw had imagined it would be. It must have been at least fifteen thousand tons. Benny followed the car in front of him into the bowels of the ferry. Three or four of the ship's crew were directing traffic and one pointed to a spot for Benny to park. They grabbed their overnight bags from the back of the van and climbed the stairs to the upper decks. After consulting the floor plans of the various decks, they located their cabin and opened the door. The cabin was small with two bunk beds, one lower and one upper and a separate shower and toilet. Bradshaw put his bag down on the chair next to the bottom bunk.
'Home sweet home.' said Benny cheerfully, dropping his in the middle of the floor. 'Let's get a drink and a bite to eat.' suggested Benny, rubbing his fat stomach. 'I'm starvin'. And very thirsty.' he added with a laugh.

They went to the upper deck, passing the brightly lit souvenir shops on the way. The bar and restaurant area took the entire forward section of one of the ferry's upper decks. There must have been seating for three hundred people or more. They found a table next to a thick glass window overlooking the quay. Benny looked around for a waiter. He spied one serving an elderly couple at a neighbouring table and let out a loud whistle and beckoned him with his

hand. When the waiter had finished serving the old couple he came over to where Bradshaw and Benny sat. Ignoring Benny, he looked at Bradshaw and said,
'Bon soir, monsieur. Would you like to order something to drink?' Before Benny could engage in another public display of bad manners and exhibit his total lack of breeding, Bradshaw said,
'I'll have a whisky with ice and water and a beer, thanks.'
'Will that be a pint, sir.' asked the waiter. Bradshaw nodded.
'Yes thanks.' he said.
'Better make it two,' interrupted Benny. 'I'm bleedin' thirsty.' The waiter permitted his eyebrows to raise a little before looking at Bradshaw for confirmation. Bradshaw nodded at the waiter.
'Very good sir.' he acknowledged and left for the bar. He returned a short time later and placed the drinks on the table. In the time it took Bradshaw to take out his wallet and pay the waiter, Benny had gulped down the first pint and had his fat paws around the second. The waiter took the empty glass and left.
'That's better.' said Benny cheerfully, wiping his mouth with the back of his hand. 'Old man Crookes gives me a few quid for booze, so we might as well make the most of it.'

In the centre of the deck, waiters were laying out a vast spread of food. Everything from cold meats to prawns and crab, soups, several different kinds of bread, roasts – beef, lamb, chicken and pork, all types of vegetables, salads, sweets and puddings, the list went on.
'The food looks good.' remarked Bradshaw.

'A bit fancy for me,' said Benny, taking another gulp of his beer, 'give me plain normal food any day.'
'Well I'm going to enjoy it.' replied Bradshaw. He helped himself to the buffet with enthusiasm. Benny steered clear of anything that wasn't sausages, mashed potatoes or gravy. Whist they were eating, Bradshaw felt a slight vibration. The ferry's engines were springing into life and they were about to leave port. Slowly the wharf and the ferry parted company and gradually the faint lights of Portsmouth grew smaller and smaller as the ferry crept out into the Solent.

After the meal they retired to one of several bars that were dotted around the decks. Benny ordered a round and they settled in for the crossing. It would take about ten hours to reach St Malo. Actually the trip was far shorter, but as they would only dock in France at seven o'clock the following morning, the ferry would spend a large part of the night zigzagging across the English Channel. They sat with their drinks and made small talk; little else was possible with Benny. About half an hour later, they were joined by two rough looking types. One was short and skinny with a bad complexion and equally bad teeth, the other overweight like Benny but with more of hoodlum appearance; tattoos covered his neck and forearms. They turned out to be acquaintances of Benny's he had met on previous trips.
'Now we can get down to some serious drinkin.' said Benny, again wiping his mouth with the back of his hand, this time in eager anticipation of the drinking bout that was to follow. He introduced Bradshaw to his two friends and ordered another round of drinks. Bradshaw nodded at the

newcomers who grabbed their pint glasses and downed half the contents in one gulp. The fat tattooed one let out a loud, appreciative belch.

'Better out than in.' he laughed and belched again. Bradshaw looked out of the window. Lights appeared on the starboard side of the ferry. A few at first, then more and more; the Isle of Wight.

'I'm going out on the deck for a while.' he said. 'I'll catch up with you later.'

'Don't take too long,' laughed Benny, 'or all the booze will be gone.' He laughed some more and so did his two drinking partners.

Bradshaw stood on the starboard deck for a good quarter of an hour watching the Isle of Wight pass slow by. The lights were now becoming fewer and fewer as though someone was turning them off one by one. It's not unlike life, he thought. The same as life's opportunities; they shine for a little while and then fade and disappear if not seized at the moment of offering. 'Not unlike my own life.' he said softly to himself, reflecting on his current financial status. As the last of the lights disappeared, Bradshaw went down to his cabin. He wasn't in the mood for Benny and his mates. He went into the cabin and climbed onto the top bunk; Benny would be too fat and too drunk to even attempt it; he'd be lucky to make the bottom one. He pulled the blanket over himself and fell into a fitful sleep. Sometime during the night he heard Benny stumble through the cabin door and fall heavily on the bunk below. He turned over and went back to sleep.

Bradshaw awoke in the morning just after six. He showered and shaved and after several unsuccessful tries, managed to get Benny to his feet. The ferry docked promptly at seven and Bradshaw and Benny joined the queue of cars disembarking.

St Malo is an ancient port city on the north coast of Brittany, with ancient stonewalls built for protection against invaders, and buildings dating back centuries. It's what the travel brochures would call picturesque. 'I don't feel well.' said Benny, driving off the ferry and though the streets of St Malo. Bradshaw just hoped that Benny would stay on the right side of the road, literally. They were not in England now. Somehow Benny managed and they proceeded out of town without incident in a northeasterly direction. Benny was unusually subdued.

They passed through a small village that could best be described as quaint. It appeared deserted except for an old man who sat alone under a tree in the town square. The next village, and the one after that were the same; deserted except for an old man sitting all by himself. It seemed to Bradshaw to be the same old man in every town. Maybe quaint was an apt description after all. About mid morning they stopped in one small town where there was more sign of life by now and purchased some jambon and fromage – ham and cheese, and a long French roll, one orange juice and a large coke. Benny pulled the van over to the side of the road a couple of kilometres outside of town. They both ate hungrily and Benny glugged on the coke. He belched several times.

'That's better.' he remarked. It appeared that he must have taken lessons from his fat friend the previous evening. With breakfast over, they resumed their journey. The food seemed to have improved Benny's disposition for shortly after they were back on the road, he was his normal talkative self.

'You left early last night.' he said, almost making a question out of it.

'Well you and your two buddies looked like you were settling in for a long session and to put it bluntly, I just don't have the spare money or the inclination to sit in pubs all night long.' Benny was silent for a few moments and then he said,

'Then when I wanted you to help me with that stuff the other weekend, why did you say no? You'd a made a few quid then.'

''That's stealing Benny and I'm not interested in that sort of thing.'

'But I keep tellin' you everyone's got a fiddle goin' on somewhere.' Benny replied indignantly. 'I told you 'bout old man Crookes. He bribes someone at the council to get the contract from them. Been doin' for years he 'as. Not the only people he bribes either. I know, I've seen him. Where d'ya think he got all his money from? – being honest? Not bleedin' likely. That's why him and his sister fight all the time. She don't approve. But why are you worried? All them politicians and businessmen are all crooks as well. It's on the news all the time. If they can do it, why can't we. And they get hundreds of times more than us, thousands. We just make a few quid here and there, they make millions. They're all the same. They're no better than us – just richer that's all.'

'It's still stealing Benny which ever way you look at it, and no amount of rationalising will change it.'

'Yeah, well I don't care. Least I can have a few beers when I want to.'

'Where are we going to buy the cigarettes and booze?' asked Bradshaw, changing the subject.

'Oh, we'll get all the stuff in Caen just before we get back on the ferry. The ferry only leaves at four this afternoon, so we've got all day. Might as well take our time.'

'Why do we catch the ferry to St Malo and drive all the way to Caen? Why not just get back on the ferry at St Malo or go straight to Caen? Apart from enjoying the French countryside, it doesn't seem to make much sense to me.'

'Well, ya' see it's this way,' explained Benny, 'we get back to England earlier this way and there's no chance of getting the same customs guys as we got last night 'cos it's a different shift. If we went back from St Malo, we'd get the same customs guys and they might remember that when we left, we were empty – that we had nothin' to deliver in France. They might figure we just came over to by the fags and booze, if you know what I mean.' Tentatively he added, 'That's the way old man Crookes wants it done – it's his idea, know what I mean?'

'No, I don't know what you mean. You told me that this was strictly legal, that there was no funny business going on.' Bradshaw snapped. Benny sensed a note of anger rising in Bradshaw's voice. Hurriedly he sought to calm the situation.

'There ain't no funny business.' he said hastily. 'Look, accordin' to the law in the UK, you can only buy enough fags and booze for personal use, otherwise ya' got to pay tax on it. That's why I brought you along. If there's two of us, then it looks better. If I go by myself, then it looks like I've bought more than just for me. This van holds a bleedin' lot you know. You can get enough fags in there to give half the country lung cancer.' Benny waited for Bradshaw's reaction and was surprised when he got none. 'You ain't angry are you?' he asked after a few seconds

'No, Benny, I'm not angry. Just let me get this one hundred percent clear in my mind. What you're saying is that anyone can buy as much alcohol and as many cigarettes as he wants, as long as it's for personal use, is that correct?' Benny nodded his head,

'Yeah, that's right.'

'How do the customs decide what is for personal use and what isn't?'

'Depends on their mood.' replied Benny, relieved that Bradshaw wasn't angry. "The law says they've got to prove that it's not for personal use, but sometimes they just confiscate the stuff. I think they keep it for themselves. Told you everyone's got a fiddle.' Bradshaw ignored the last comment.

'So if they can't prove it's not for personal use, legally they can do nothing about it?'

'Legally yeah, but like I said ...

'And how much cheaper is it in France than in England?' interrupted Bradshaw.

'Hell, it's a lot cheaper here. The Froggies 'ave got that right at least. Old man Crookes will make himself a few hundred quid out 'a this lot. He's paying me two hundred.'

'So this load we're going to pick up isn't just for personal use then?' Benny looked a bit sheepish and shrugged his shoulders defensively.

'Some of it is.' he said finally.

'So who does he sell the rest to? His friends?' enquired Bradshaw as casually as he could.

'He keeps some for himself like I said, but most of it he sells it to a mate of his – Errol Chong the Chinaman. I dunno what the Chinaman does with the stuff, but I hear he's got contacts if you know what I mean.'

'Hm.' replied Bradshaw slowly, 'I know what you mean Benny.' It was mid afternoon when they arrived in the river port city of Caen situated on the Normandy coast. Caen was the scene of fierce fighting between the Germans and the Allies in June and July 1944 and is also the burial place of William the Conqueror. Benny stopped the van outside a large supermarket that was surrounded by several other shops of varying sizes.

'Right,' he said 'let's go shoppin'. There's a few places we got to go to get the best price, otherwise old man Crookes has a fit.' They went into five or six shops, all promising the best prices in town. In spite of his boast to Paul Crookes that he had memorised the shopping list, Benny methodically checked the prices of items on a piece of paper he produced from his pocket.

'Right, he said at last, 'we can get all this lot here and the rest at the first shop we went to.' They loaded the van with cases of red and white wines, whisky and vodka. A couple of cases of gin were added for good measure as well as half a dozen cases of brandy. 'That should do it.' said Benny, looking satisfied with himself.

'What about the cigarettes?' asked Bradshaw.

'We'll get those on the ferry.' explained Benny, 'You can't buy fags in the shops in France. Only in those little *tabacs* they have all over the place, but they don't 'av large quantities. Anyway, they're cheaper on the ferry.'

Shortly after, they boarded the ferry, wandered up to the recreation deck and purchased several thousand cigarettes from the bar. The man serving didn't appear to think such large purchases were unusual and the whole transaction was completed without incident. Bradshaw noticed this with interest.
'They don't seem concerned about selling such large quantities,' Bradshaw remarked to Benny.
'No, they couldn't care less; why should they?' The ferry left Caen on time and arrived back at Portsmouth later that evening. The drive back to Hounslow was uneventful and it was just after ten when they arrived back at Crookes Transport.
'No one here.' said Benny irritably, 'We'll have to go round to the Chinaman's I suppose. Can't leave the van full of this stuff overnight.' It took another ten or twelve minutes of driving up and down side streets before arriving at Errol Chong's. Bradshaw concentrated on remembering the way. Finally they pulled to a stop at the end of a poorly lit narrow street. There was a light on in what appeared to look like a dilapidated office and Benny knocked loudly on the door. A short man of Chinese descent appeared.
'Benny,' he said with delight, 'you've bought my stuff. You make an old man happy. Please unload in the storeroom.' He glanced at the van. 'I see you got someone to help you.' After two or three attempts, Benny managed to turn the van around and reversed up to the double doors of the

storeroom that was alongside the Chinaman's office. Errol Chong was a man of indeterminate age; he could have been fifty or he could have been seventy. He gave Bradshaw a slight bow when Benny introduced him. Bradshaw nodded.

'You put the stuff along this wall here, Benny.' but made no effort to assist with the unloading. Twenty minutes later the van was empty and all its contents were neatly stacked where Errol Chong wanted them.

'Got to get you to sign for it,' said Benny. A quick stock take was done, a signature obtained and everyone was happy.

'I give Mr Crookes money tomorrow.' said Errol Chong. 'When you go again Benny?'

'I dunno,' replied Benny, 'when Mr Crookes tells me I s'ppose. Could be a week, could be a month, you know what I mean.'

'I take as much as you can bring Benny. Everyday you bring, everyday I take.' laughed the Chinaman. 'You know I have contacts. You bring me more Benny.' As Benny drove him back to his flat, Bradshaw asked,

'Did he mean what he said; that he will take as much as you can deliver?'

'That old Chinaman can never get enough booze and fags. He knows lots of people up in London with restaurants, nightclubs and corner shops. Why?'

No reason.' answered Bradshaw. 'Just curious.' After Benny had dropped him off, Bradshaw spent the next hour or so with pen, paper and his calculator. Tomorrow he would take a walk passed the used car garages, and then have a chat with Errol Chong.

The visit to Errol Chong's proved to be fruitful. Chong remembered Bradshaw from the previous evening and welcomed him politely.

'Mr Chong,' asked Bradshaw, 'last night you said that you could handle as much cigarettes and booze as we could deliver. Did you mean that?'

'Oh, yes,' replied the Chinaman, his eyes lighting up, 'I take all you bring.'

'Okay, now how much will you pay me?'

'You come to office, we discuss.' offered Chong and led the way into his office. Half an hour later, after a mixture of bargaining and negotiating, offers and counter offers, Bradshaw emerged with a list of prices Chong was prepared to pay and another list of items his "clients" preferred.

He left Mr Chong's in high spirits. His plans were starting to taking shape in his mind as he walked back towards his flat. After some lunch he would look for a suitable vehicle. There were several used car garages within walking distance of Bradshaw's flat and he passed by all of them, noting prices and the general condition of medium sized vans. There was one in particular that appealed and his limited finances could afford. He would come back during the week when the office was open.

~ Chapter 5 ~

Two events of significance happened to Bradshaw during the course of the following week. Firstly, after some prolonged haggling, he purchased the van he had seen the previous Sunday. He ended up paying only slightly more than he intended, but the vehicle was in good condition and had done a relatively low mileage. It would be ready for him to collect on the following Monday afternoon. Secondly, on the Wednesday evening, he and Benny had just returned to Crookes Transport when he was summons to the office; Miss Crookes wished to see him. He knocked on her door and entered. She looked up from her desk and said,

'Ah, Mr Bradshaw, thanks for coming. The reason I wanted to speak to is that I want some furniture taken down to my cottage on the coast on Saturday morning. Would you be interested in some overtime?'

'Yes I would,' replied Bradshaw, 'As long as I'm paid tax-free.'

‘That won’t be a problem.’ she agreed.
‘Where do I have to collect the furniture from?’
‘From my house at eight o’clock. Here’s the address.’ she said handing him a piece of paper with her address written on it in bold handwriting. Bradshaw looked at the paper and then at Suzanne Crookes.
‘I’ll see you at eight o’clock on Saturday morning then.’
‘Good. You can bring the van that you and Benny use. Goodnight Mr Bradshaw.’
‘Goodnight Miss Crookes.’

Bradshaw arrived at Suzanne Crookes house at precisely eight o’clock on Saturday morning. As he walked towards her front door, it opened and Suzanne Crookes stepped out. She was dressed in a pair of faded denim jeans and a sweater. Her hair was loose and hung down just below her shoulders.
‘Good morning.’ she said brightly. ‘Right on time I see.’
‘Good morning Miss Crookes.’ replied Bradshaw.
‘My name’s Suzanne. We’re not at work now, Mr Bradshaw,’ she said with mocking chastisement.
“May I call you James or is it Jim or Jimmy?’ It was the first time Bradshaw had seen her smile.
‘James is just fine.’ he answered, returning her smile. ‘Right now, where’s all this furniture you want taken to the coast?’
‘There’s just my lounge suite and a couple of chairs. I’ll give you a hand to load the van.’ An involuntary expression of doubt betrayed Bradshaw’s thoughts. ‘Don’t look at me like that,’ she said, ‘I’m not made of porcelain. I can lift

a chair or two without breaking.' And so within twenty minutes the van was loaded and true to her word, Suzanne Crookes hadn't broken.

'Okay,' said Bradshaw, 'where are we going with all this stuff?'

'How about you drive and I navigate?'

'Sounds good to me.' replied Bradshaw opening the passenger's door for Suzanne Crookes. He then walked around to the driver's side, climbed in behind the wheel and started the engine.

'Which way navigator?' he asked. They headed onto the M25, that vast motorway that circumnavigates Greater London and then turned off onto the A21 towards Hastings. It was a glorious summer's day and the green countryside flashed passed. The sun seemed to lend an ambiance of prosperity wherever it shone. People everywhere seemed infused with a sense of purpose; the lethargy of winter hibernation discarded. It felt good to be alive. At first they exchanged pleasantries and made idle chatter before Suzanne asked in a more serious note,

'Why do you drive a van for Crookes Transport?'

'I don't,' he replied, 'I unload a van for Crookes Transport.' Noticing that she didn't seem amused at his answer, he added, 'I needed a job. I have to earn money and the way the job market is at the moment, a male over the age of forty, let alone over fifty, is not a sought after commodity, so I take what I can get. Why do you ask?

'Because you don't fit the typical profile of our employees. You're intelligent and from what I hear very honest. I'm sure you could do a lot better than drive a van. I mean unload a van.'

'That's what I thought as well, but it doesn't seem that the captains of industry agree with either of us.' he replied with a tinge of sarcasm

'You sound rather bitter.' It was more a question than a statement. Keeping one eye on the road and one eye on Suzanne Crookes, he said as unemotionally as he could,

'I am to a certain extent. At the age of almost fifty, I stopped work, took a full time computer course, studied hard, passed all my exams and qualified, got a job at far less money than I was accustomed to earning, gained practical experience in the real world and now whenever I apply for a position in the IT industry, I'm looked at like I'm a doddering old fool. Meanwhile, while I'm battling financially, there's the likes of Benny who has a council house that is subsidised heavily by the taxpayer, which means by you and me and millions like us. In addition to that I also have to support his slut of a sister and her dysfunctional litter and thousands of other parasites just like her.' By this stage Bradshaw was spitting out his words as though they had lain dormant within him for too long and had now found an avenue of release. 'I work to support myself,' he continued, 'and to be able to take care of myself in my old age, so that I'm not a burden on anyone else. But what chance do I have when the damn government steals at least sixty percent of what I earn in the form of taxation and hands it out to any lame duck that comes along with a begging bowl. Yes, I am bitter, but even more so, I'm angry. And believe me, things are going to change in the very near future.' Suzanne remained silent, digesting what she had just heard. 'Don't worry,' he added, 'I'm not going to rob a bank or anything like that.' He forced a laugh trying to ease the tension. Finally she looked at him and asked,

'Just what are you going to do then?' He looked at her thoughtfully before answering.

'I've bought a second hand van which I pick up next week and then every weekend I'm going to France on the Friday night ferry, buy cigarettes and wine and spirits and bring them back here. I've got someone who'll take the lot off my hands and if I can keep doing that for a while, I'll be able to save some money and become financially independent again.'

'That's illegal.' she said simply.

'It's not immoral,' he replied. 'and that's all that concerns me anymore. I'm sick to death of these ridiculous rules and laws that make no sense whatsoever; that are there simply to penalise anyone who shows any ambition or initiative; that are there to punish rather than reward anyone who is prepared to work hard or put in long hours to better himself and his family. I am not a slave to toil day and night for the benefit of some unknown ingrate; so some lazy unambitious layabouts can have designer hairdos, tattoos on their faces and earrings in their snouts, all at my expense.'

'I agree with your sentiments entirely,' said Suzanne, 'but that's the way the system works. And it's getting worse.' she added.

'Of course it is.' replied Bradshaw. 'If the voters keep electing these damn left wing governments, what else can you expect? That's why I left England twenty odd years ago and one of the reasons I came back was because I thought a lot of this socialist hypocrisy had ended during the Thatcher years. I thought that the economy was leaning more towards a free market system than it was back in the sixties and seventies.'

'Oh, it did. Things improved tremendously under Margaret Thatcher, but ever since the Labour Government regained office, things have gone downhill again. Taxes are up, services are down, there's more and more intrusion in every aspect of everyone's life and there doesn't seem to be any light at the end of the tunnel. No one seems to be happy with the way things are, but somehow they got voted back in at the last election'

'Well,' replied Bradshaw, 'there's no effective opposition. It's about time the Conservatives woke up to themselves and provided that opposition. They need to determine exactly what it is they're trying to conserve and why. It can't be the status quo – that's been socialism for more than half a century. Ideologically they've lost their way. Half of them are nothing better than rabid socialists themselves and the other half are confused. They don't know what they stand for anymore. All we hear from them are meaningless platitudes. They've got to decide what it is they stand for and then they need to explain *morally* why their beliefs and policies are correct, and explain this in clear, concise language, so that those who still vote against them will no longer be able to doubt their own lack of moral status. But what are they doing at the moment? Mimicking the Labour Party. Anything the Labour Party says they want to do, the Conservatives response is: "That's what we want to do as well, only we want to do it differently." How can they seriously expect to win an election with that approach? Moral cowardice is not usually a source of inspiration. Anyway, I am not a politician. Nobody listens to anything I say; I'm just a doddering old fool, didn't you know? So I'll just get on with my own life and do what I have to do to get by without infringing on anyone else's rights and without being a parasite.'

'Quite a speech for an unloader of vans. Maybe you should become a politician.' said Suzanne jokingly.

'No thanks, I still have too much self-respect for that.'

'See, I told you that you weren't like our typical employee.'

When they reached Hastings, what was left of an early morning mist was vaguely discernable.

'Left at the next turning.' directed Suzanne. Bradshaw swung the van onto the road that led to the village of Fairlight. Suzanne Crookes' cottage lay in a sheltered dip half a mile inland from the coast. Its white walls were topped off with a thatch roof. It was small, but comfortable, with three bedrooms and a neat garden at the front and back.

'This is it.' said Suzanne. 'This is where I come for peace and quiet and get away from the rat race.'

Between them they unloaded the furniture and carried it inside.

'I think some lunch would be a good idea.' suggested Suzanne when they had finally brought the lounge suite to rest in its most suitable position. 'There's a good restaurant not far from here overlooking the sea.'

'Sounds good to me.' replied Bradshaw. 'This sea air has given me an appetite.' The restaurant was about half full and they managed to find a quiet table with a view of Rye Bay and the English Channel. The waves crashed unmercifully on the rocks below and the seagulls squawked noisily overhead. The mist of earlier had completely lifted and several ships could be seen slowly bobbing their way up and down one of the busiest waterways in the world. A waitress brought them a menu and they ordered fresh seafood and a bottle of cold wine that Suzanne recommended. They sipped their wine, enjoying the splendid view and waited for their meal to arrive.

'How did you get into the transport business?' asked Bradshaw. Suzanne put down her glass before replying.

'Crookes Transport was started by my father many years ago. He died when I was twenty-five. I had just finished a business degree at university. In his will he left the business to my brother Paul and me. Paul had been working in the business with my father since he left school. Paul wasn't academically inclined.' she added as by way of an explanation. 'So Paul received sixty percent and I got forty percent plus the cottage down here. My father was old fashioned in some ways. Maybe he thought that the man should have the larger share, or perhaps it was because Paul is five years older than me and had been working in the business for a few years. Anyway that's the way it worked out. We've done reasonably well, but it's a hard business to be in; there's plenty of competition and some of the opposition are, well, they're not exactly ethical.' Her voice held a note of disappointment. Bradshaw remembered what Benny had said about Paul Crookes, bribery and the local council.

'From what I can see in the newspapers,' he replied, 'there seems to be an awful lot of corruption around, and not just in the transport business'

'My father was an extremely ethical man, James. He did not approve of anything that was remotely underhanded. He would sooner forego business than be involved in something that wasn't completely above board. Paul and I don't always see eye to eye with regard to some of his business tactics. I'm sure my father would turn in his grave if he knew, but that seems to be the way of the world these days. All you have to do is obey the eleventh commandment: "Thou shalt not get caught".'

'Sadly you're right,' said Bradshaw, 'but the way I see it is, if I only claim that which I have earned and do not expect the unearned in any way, shape or form, then I can hold my head high, and that's all that counts. Let the liars and cheats get on with their lying and cheating as long as they don't lie and cheat with me.' The waiter approached and placed their meals in front of them. They touched glasses and Bradshaw proposed a toast to "more honest days"

'To more honest days.' said Suzanne.

~ Chapter 6 ~

The following Monday afternoon Bradshaw left work promptly at five and hurried on foot to the car dealers and after a brisk twenty-minute walk arrived just before they closed for the day. As he walked to the office, the salesman he had dealt with came out to greet him.

'Your van's ready Mr Bradshaw. I've had it checked out. Everything's a hundred percent. Come and see for yourself.' he said, leading Bradshaw to a white Ford Transit van. He walked over to it and gave it a quick inspection. The van had been cleaned and the tyres were in good condition; there should be plenty of mileage left in them, he thought. Satisfied that everything was in order, Bradshaw signed the release papers, escaped from the salesman and drove away. He felt better than he had for some time. This van was his means to free himself from his current life of enforced servitude and eternal poverty. This coming weekend he would go to France. It was time to start working for himself instead of everyone else.

Wednesday afternoon was a cold and wet. An unexpected cold front was sweeping across the country. Bradshaw and Benny had collected another delivery from Crookes Transport. The heater in the van wasn't working and they were both shivering with cold. Benny was driving as usual and Bradshaw was thumbing through the delivery schedule. As Benny turned off the main road, Bradshaw said, 'You're going the wrong way Benny, we should have gone straight on back there.
I've got to go to my sister's house quickly. It's just down here. I've got to give her somethin.' It won't take long.'

A few minutes later, Benny pulled over to the kerb.
'This is 'er place here.' he said pointing to a new two-storey house. 'Come on in. We'll get a cup of tea and warm up a bit.' Reluctantly Bradshaw followed Benny to the front door. Through the closed door they could hear the sound of screaming children. Benny knocked loudly. An overweight scruffy looking woman in her early thirties opened the door. A surly looking girl of about thirteen accompanied her. The woman's unkempt hair was a mixture of colours, mainly purples and reds. She had a tattoo of a five-pointed star on her left cheek, three small silver earrings in one eyebrow and a large golden colour one through her nostril. What were left of her teeth were pointed and uneven. She was chewing gum with her open mouth. She

reminded Bradshaw of a cow chewing its cud; only the cow had more appeal. She looked Bradshaw up and down without a word and turned to her brother.

'D'ya bring the stuff?' she asked. Children were still screaming in the background. Before Benny could reply, she turned her head and shrieked, 'Shut up you lot. I'm bleedin' sick and tired of all your crap.'

'Yeah, 'ere it is.' said Benny, handing her a small package wrapped in a brown paper bag as they pushed their way along the cluttered passage. 'This is James.' he added pointing at Bradshaw. 'This is me sister Wanda.'

'Whatever.' she replied. 'I told you lot to shut up.' she screamed again in the direction of the living room.

'How about a cup of tea?' asked Benny. 'We're freezing. The bleedin' 'eater in the van's packed up.'

'Linda, put the kettle on will ya.' Wanda ordered the surly looking girl. 'Ya uncle Benny and 'is mate want some tea.' Without uttering a word the girl shuffled her way silently to what Bradshaw presumed was the kitchen. They went into the living room and were greeted by the sight of four neglected urchins. They ranged in age from about three years old up to ten or eleven. Their clothes were dirty and toys were strewn all over the floor. The television blared but no one was watching it. The furniture was obviously brand new, but it already showed the scars of misuse. On the coffee table stood a half finished bottle of vodka and an almost full glass. The chairs were littered with cheap magazines.

'Grab a seat.' said Wanda. 'Chuck that stuff on the floor if it's in the way.' She unwrapped the paper bag Benny had given her. It contained marijuana and she spent the couple of minutes engrossed in rolling herself a joint. When she finished, she produced a cigarette lighter from among the mess on the floor and lit up. She sat back in her chair a drew heavily on the joint. She turned her head towards the kitchen. 'Where's that bleedin' tea?' she bellowed so as to be heard over the moronic sound of the rap music that blared from the kitchen at ear shattering volume. 'Bring two cups 'd'ya' hear me.' In between drags she gulped from the glass of vodka. 'I fought it were the welfare when you knocked so bleedin' loud. They're lookin' for me again 'cos the kids ain't been going to school. How can I make 'em go if they don't wanna? They never listen to a fing I say.' Linda returned from the kitchen carrying a tray containing a teapot, two dirty looking mugs, a carton of milk and a sugar bowl. A solitary spoon stuck out of the sugar and some milk had been spilt on the tray. She deposited it on the coffee table and without saying a word turned to leave the room. 'And what's wrong with you? Don't yer say hello to yer uncle Benny no more?' yelled Wanda. Without turning her head, the girl insolently mumbled something that was barely audible and walked out of the living room. 'Dunno what I'm goin' to do with 'er. Never listens to a fing I say. Little know-all bitch.' She pointed to the teapot. 'Help yerselves. I ain't yer bleedin' slave.' Benny poured himself a mug, slopping tea on the tray, and then proceeded to slurp it greedily. Bradshaw declined with a shake of his head and took a wary look around the room. It was like being in a cave with a hag from Hell and her tribe of untamed savages. By comparison, the cold of the van was increasingly inviting and Bradshaw was not slow to leave when Benny told his sister they had to be going.

'It's not fair,' said Benny as they drove away, 'the welfare's always pickin' on er' 'cos the kids won't do as they're told. What can she do if they never listen to a fing she says? And it's worse now Linda got caught. It wasn't 'er fault. She's only a kid and she wanted some extra money for clothes and stuff. You know what I mean.'

'No, I don't know what you mean.' replied Bradshaw and regretted it the second he'd opened his mouth as Benny seized the opportunity to embark on yet another discourse on the "unfair" fortunes of the Barrett family. Apparently Linda had decided that a career in the world of drugs was full of promise. She had been caught selling drugs to some of her fellow pupils and duly expelled from her school. As the law determined that it was her right to an education, but because she had proven herself unfit to associate with children of her own age, the courts in their wisdom had deemed she would receive the balance of her education from a private tutor. As the nearest suitable tutor was several miles away and was not on a bus route, the lovely Linda was ferried back and forth each day by taxi. Naturally this was done at the taxpayer's expense. Barely able to control his rising anger, Bradshaw forced himself to listen to Benny's monologue in icy silence.

'So this is what *my* hard earned money goes on after the government has stolen it.' Bradshaw fumed to himself. The whole scenario was ridiculous. Why should an ill-mannered surly brat who sold drugs to her school friends be chauffeur driven around the countryside to receive private, one-on-one tuition, whilst honest, hard-working children received nothing? If this was "social justice" as the liberals liked to call it, then he wanted no part of it.

The week seemed to go by at a snail's pace but finally Friday afternoon arrived and immediately after finishing up at work, Bradshaw threw a small overnight bag into his van and set off to Portsmouth. On his long nightly journeys to Cheltenham, he had mentally planned his trip meticulously. During the week he had purchased a map of a France from Mr Thomas' shop and had spent his lunch breaks studying the various routes he could take. That morning before work, he had stopped in at Mr Thomas' shop and bought a packet of popular cigarettes. He opened the packet, removed two or three cigarettes which he threw away and placed the packet on the dashboard of his van. If any customs agent stopped him, at least it would look as though Bradshaw was a smoker.

He boarded the same ferry he and Benny had taken, enjoyed his evening meal and then went straight to his cabin. He wanted and early night; there was a lot to do the following day. The ferry berthed promptly at seven the next morning and Bradshaw drove through St Malo a short distance before pulling over to the side of the road. Driving on the opposite of the road was a new experience; one that took a little getting used to. Driving in a straight line was no problem, but when Bradshaw turned a corner or approached a roundabout, thirty-five years of habit required a great deal of concentration to overcome. He opened his road map of France and double-checked his route. On this trip there would be no messing around nursing Benny and his hangover. Bradshaw had decided to spend as much time as possible shopping around in order to get the cheapest prices. This was business a trip, not a pleasure cruise. He stopped at various supermarkets comparing prices.

This trip would mainly be an exploratory one; next time he would know where the best bargains were to be bought. Many of the shops now had their own Internet sites where they advertised current specials. Bradshaw made a note of the addresses for future reference. He chose a different route from the one Benny had taken, which took him through larger towns where there were more and bigger supermarkets to choose from and hopefully cheaper prices. At last when his van was full, he completed the remainder of the journey to Caen.

He filled the van with diesel before boarding the ferry. Diesel was quite a bit cheaper on the French side of the Channel. The Labour government back in Westminster had long since decided that the British motorist was their new milch cow and milked them without respite . On the ferry he purchased his stock of cigarettes, buying only the same brand as the open packet he had left on the dashboard of his van. The English Channel was having and off day and Bradshaw and the rest of the passengers were glad to set their feet on dry land when they eventually docked at Portsmouth. As Bradshaw approached the customs officials, he experienced a feeling that was a combination of apprehension and defiance, though mainly defiance. Probably because the weather had turned to a rainy squall, he passed through customs with no more than a nod from the rain soaked officer. So far, so good.

The drive home took longer than expected; the bad weather had followed him from the coast and it was gone ten o'clock when Bradshaw finally pulled into the parking area behind his flat. There were three garages there and Bradshaw had negotiated earlier in the week with Mr Thomas, the shopkeeper, to rent one for a modest sum. He drove his van into the garage and securely bolted and locked the door with a chain and a substantial padlock. After a hot shower he went straight to bed.

He arose early the next morning, phoned Errol Chong and arranged to meet him later that morning. Mr Chong was happy to see him and after the customary greetings, Bradshaw exchanged his recent purchases for an envelope containing the agreed amount of cash.
'You bring again very soon James.'
'Same time next week Mr Chong.' Apparently nobody referred to Errol Chong other than as Mr Chong. They shook hands, Mr Chong bowed and Bradshaw left.

Back at his flat, Bradshaw turned on his computer. He quickly prepared a spreadsheet detailing all the costs of his trip to France and in another column the amount he had received from Mr Chong. The difference, his profit. The word sounded almost magical – profit, not salary, not wages, not some pittance left over after the government had robbed him blind, but sweet, glorious profit, tax free profit. He continued his calculations. If he could make fifty trips a year, together with his savings, he could afford to buy a flat of his own or maybe even a small house in about four or five years time. After a further five years, if all went well, he would also have a small nest egg for his retirement. Five hundred trips, virtually one per week for ten years; an awful lot. 'Well, only four hundred and ninety nine to go.' he thought to himself. It was then that Bradshaw made the decision to vary the options of getting to France. To go via Portsmouth every week could arouse suspicion amongst the customs officials. Checking on the Internet revealed that ferries and the Channel Tunnel were available from Dover and a ferry service from Newhaven in the summer season. Poole and Weymouth were also possibilities but they both involved increased driving distance and Bradshaw wanted to preserve his van for as long as he could, so he ruled them both out. The costs varied between the different routes, so Bradshaw created another spreadsheet to calculate the financial implications and by how much his profit would be affected. Fortunately in the overall picture, and for the sake of safety, it wasn't a major consideration. Things at last were starting to look up.

~ Chapter 7 ~

For the next few months, each Friday afternoon, Bradshaw left work promptly, went back to his flat, showered, changed his clothes and set off for France. He varied his route and experienced very few difficulties. Occasionally an over zealous customs official would look inside his van. One even insinuated that if his load was for personal consumption, then Bradshaw surely had a drinking problem 'Not to mention lung cancer.' laughed Bradshaw as he drove away. As ever, Mr Chong was glad to relieve him of his stock and always had a brown envelope containing cash waiting for him. This was free trade in its purest form – no third party stealing an unearned portion.

At work, Suzanne Crookes treated him in a businesslike manner, and without showing any favouritism, ensured that he was offered overtime whenever it was available. The nightly run to Cheltenham had finished, so Bradshaw accepted gratefully, as overtime was often paid on a cash basis with no deductions for tax. Slowly his savings grew, but at a pace that would embarrass a snail.

One Tuesday morning as Bradshaw was clocking in, Suzanne Crookes approached him.
'I need some more furniture taken down to my cottage this weekend. A table and some of chairs. I also want to paint a couple of the rooms. Are you available to give me a hand?'
'Well, ' replied Bradshaw, 'I was planning to go to France.'
'I hear that you've been going to France every week for the past three of four months. A break will do you good and I'll pay you the usual overtime rate. In cash of course.' she added persuasively. It was true, Bradshaw hadn't had a break in months and anyway, his van was overdue for a service. This was a good opportunity to have it done.
'As long as it's tax free how can I refuse an offer like that?' he said, 'Eight o'clock Saturday morning at your house?
'Eight o'clock Saturday morning at my house, and it will be tax free.'

Old Mr Thomas had referred Bradshaw to a local mechanic called Nick King. 'He does a good job and doesn't rip you off like a lot of places.' he had told him. So Bradshaw made the necessary arrangements with Nick King and dropped his van off at King's workshop after work that Friday. He arose early on Saturday morning, collected a Crookes Transport van and drove to Suzanne Crookes' house. She was waiting for him and together they quickly loaded the furniture and some tins of paint.

Winter was approaching and the van's heater and windscreen demister worked overtime. The weather at the coast was bleak. They put on thick coats, scarves and gloves as a cold, wet wind battered them. Between them they carried the table and chairs inside as quickly as possible. Suzanne heated some soup whilst Bradshaw brought in the tins of paint. Suzanne turned on the heater and after greedily attacking the steaming hot soup, they started to warm up.

'Right,' said Bradshaw, 'I'd better start earning my money. I'll get on with the painting.' They started in the small dining room. They moved the furniture into the living room before laying old sheets on the carpet to protect it. Armed with a roller and a tray of paint each, they proceeded to repaint the walls in silence. A radio played music softly in the background. Suzanne seemed absorbed in some secret thought as she applied the new paint. Suddenly she put down her roller and turned around towards Bradshaw.

'Tell me, why are you so obsessed with taxation? I've heard plenty of people complain about the amount of tax they're forced to pay, but James, you seem to hate paying tax with a passion I've never seen before.' she asked. He put his roller in the paint tray before turning to face her. He said stared straight at her and said nothing for a moment or two as if contemplating the best way to reply.

'Because it's totally immoral.' he said finally. 'It's the most widespread form of slavery ever perpetuated on mankind and it goes virtually unchallenged. Even your most rabid left-wingers and evil socialists acknowledge that Man's most basic right is his right to life. Surely it must follow that Man's second most important right is to be free to support that life. It is a contradiction to have the right to life, but be denied the right to support it. Since Man must work in order to survive, he must be free to keep the product of his labour. In other words, in any society that claims to be civilised, after the right to life, the most essential rights must be properly formulated property rights. Property rights mean a man's freedom to earn, keep, use and dispose of the products of his labour as he sees fit. This is the true meaning of property rights and taxation negates that right. If anyone else can force him to act against his will in this regard, it's not property rights he has but mere privileges; and a privilege can be granted, amended or revoked at the whim of another at any time. At best, taxation is a form of involuntary servitude, which is a polite euphemism for slavery. But in reality it is nothing more than legalised theft. If the man who has earned the reward does not have absolute right to that reward, then by what moral standard can someone who has not earned it, have any right to it whatsoever?'

'Fundamental to Man's survival qua Man, is the absolute necessity for him to be free to pursue his goals, to make his own decisions as to what is his best course of action and to succeed or fail by those decisions. His very nature rebels at any attempt to use coercion or force to make him act against his own will. Without freedom Man will whither and die, or at best, merely exist in a sub human state. But he cannot live as his nature meant him to live, not in any real sense of the word if the continual threat of force hangs over his head. The fact that Man is the only species on the planet that has the faculty of volitional choice, and this volitional choice is his most basic means, in fact his only means of survival, necessitates he be free in order to exercise that choice. If he is not permitted to exercise that choice, he is no longer free; he is no longer Man; he is nothing more than a mindless beast. Since his ability to choose is by no means infallible, he must sink or swim by his own choices. He can blame no other man for his own lack of good judgement. The man who leads a fulfilling and successful life is one who makes correct choices in accordance with Man's nature: the man who leads a life of despair and frustration, is one who does not. Each and every man has to make choices; and this ironically, is the only aspect of his life about which he has no choice; the fact that he has to make choices; this is his nature. He is free to make correct choices that will lead to a life of progress and happiness, or he can make incorrect choices whereby he will self-destruct. Implicit in Man's right to freedom is his right to dispose of the rewards of his own labour as he sees fit. It is long overdue that that right be made explicit.'

'That's all well and good, but how does anyone know if his choices are correct or incorrect? Trial and error could prove disastrous.' interrupted Suzanne.

'It often does. That's the purpose of philosophy. Adopting and following the correct philosophy will lead Man to make correct decisions; a false philosophy will lead to bad decisions and his eventual destruction.'

'That's easier said the done.' she replied. 'How does one determine the correct philosophy?'

'Once again it's up to each individual to decide for himself. That's what choice is all about. But my suggestion would be to adopt a philosophy that is in accordance with, and therefore results in, Man's survival qua Man. Any philosophy that leads to his misery or his demise is surely erroneous. The situation that faces mankind today is a world virtually without any rational philosophy. Philosophy is all but dead and buried and tragically all we have left are the twin poisons of altruism and mysticism. When a country lacks a rational philosophy, it inevitably becomes morally bankrupt.'

'But we're always being told that to be altruistic is a virtue,' interrupted Suzanne again, 'and that self sacrifice is noble.'

Bradshaw rushed on as if this had been pent up inside for too long. Like a volcano that had lain dormant for too long he exploded with all the fury of a Vesuvius or an Etna.

'And who is that spouts that poison? Left wing academics hidden in their ivory towers far away from the real world, and mealy-mouthed politicians who will say anything to get a vote. It's not a question of helping others. It's a question of being **forced** to lend aid to others to your own detriment. The philosophy of altruism is the most vile, most cancerous disease that has ever been inflicted on mankind; that combined with all the various forms of mysticism, that have been forced on mankind throughout the ages. Together they have bought more injustice, more death and destruction and more human misery than all the other disasters combined since the dawn of time. Altruism is the philosophy of slavery and its physical implementation is taxation. It reduces the most able of men, the producers, to slaves and the least able to parasites. It turns the best amongst men into sacrificial animals for the benefit of the inefficient, the idle and the unambitious. And what do these producers get in return? – a deafening demand for more, that's what. Not a word of thanks, no gratitude, no appreciation, nothing, nothing but more abuse and ridicule, and even more chains, and even more lashes from the communal whip. It is the philosophy of the savage. It denies any rights to the individual and subjects him to the whim of the tribe or the state or "society" or the "common good" or some other equally meaningless cause such as "social responsibility". It has its roots in tribalism; it is anti individual and that is why the liberal left are hell bent on discrediting Man's ego. And this is all done in the name of love of mankind. And yet in reality, mankind has only advanced from the cave to the skyscraper and beyond due entirely to the incalculable genius of a hand full of men. A few individuals who dared and had the brilliance to think differently from their contemporaries. And throughout history, these men have been persecuted, tortured and even put to death, all in the name of the love of mankind. This is the ugly truth behind the evil of altruism. This is what it means for those who are able to bring man salvation, to bring him an ever and ever higher standard of living, to drag him from the Dark Ages to enlightenment. This is how your left wing liberals view these men, and this is how they now treat all men. According to them, all men are created equals. To suggest that we are all born equals is one of the biggest falsehoods and con jobs of all time. If it is true that all men are born equal, why then is it necessary to "redistribute wealth" via discriminatory taxation? If it is not true, then why perpetuate the lie? The reality is that we are not born equals and therefore we will each achieve at varying levels and receive varying rewards. The only moral sense in which it is correct to claim that we are all equals, is from a legal viewpoint. In any country that claims to be civilised, under the law, all men must be treated equally.'

'We're always told that we're so fortunate to live in free country, yet we're continually forced against our wills to pay for things we either don't want or don't use, or both.

How can that be freedom? And as for helping those who are less fortunate, surely the best method is to educate them in the ways of self reliance and to encourage them to stand on their own two feet. Merely giving one hand-out after another has failed miserably and only increases sloth. If socialism and the welfare state worked so well, why after more than half a century of it, do we still have "the poor"? Look at it this way; if I gave you twenty million pounds tomorrow, you would consider yourself rich. If I gave everyone else in the country one hundred million pounds the day after, you'd consider yourself poor. It's all relative and the Left will always find more "poor and vulnerable" people and invent ever increasing ways of stealing the property of others to "help" them. In other words, more and more taxes.'

'But the government needs money to run the country. It's got to get it from somewhere.' interjected Suzanne.

'We all need money to run our lives as well, but the vast majority of us do not go and steal it. Why does the government? Why does the government have a legal monopoly on theft? And more to the point, why should it have? The answer is, it shouldn't. Have you ever asked yourself do we need a government and if so, what is its proper function? Ninety nine percent of people have never asked themselves this question; they've just accepted the status quo and so successive governments continue to get away, literally, with daylight robbery. The answer is yes, we do need a government, for reasons I won't go into now, but the only moral function of any government is to protect the rights of its citizens, nothing else, just to protect our rights, which in essence means to protect each and every individual against the use of force by someone else. Yet what actually happens in our so-called great and enlightened democracies? It is illegal for me to use force against you or anyone else, but it's legal for the government, our supposed protector, to use force against anyone it chooses. If that's not extreme hypocrisy then I don't know what is. If governments only restricted themselves to protecting the rights of their citizens, then they would not require the vast sums of money they now devour. They would only need to provide for the armed services to protect us from foreign aggression, a judiciary to deal with those who break the country's laws and for contractual disputes and a police force to bring the criminal element to trial. That should be the extent of their influence.'

'What about education, hospitals and that sort of thing?' asked Suzanne

'What about them? Do you honestly believe that if government did not provide them they would not exist? Of course they would. Hundreds, thousands of enterprises exist independent of government. To suggest that if the government doesn't engage in a particular activity, then that activity would not exist is utter nonsense. It's the same as saying if the government didn't produce shoes, we'd all be bare-footed or if they didn't provide bread we'd all go hungry. Such a notion is more than ridiculous. And as you well know, private enterprise provides better quality at lower prices than any government can in any field of production. By and large the schools and hospitals that are provided by the private sector are far superior to those provided by government.'

'That's true,' she answered, 'but they're also more expensive. A lot of poorer people can't afford to go to private schools and hospitals.'

'Oh, really,' he countered, 'let's look for a moment at the things they can and do afford. They can afford designer haircuts, they can afford to tattoo themselves, they can afford to have earrings in their snouts, they can afford to sit in the pub and drink themselves into a coma, they can afford to smoke themselves to death, they can afford a least one overseas holiday to Spain every year, and you want to tell me they can't afford to educate their children or they can't afford medical treatment? The vast majority can afford it, but their priorities are wrong. What happens in reality is that you and I, and millions like us, pay for their haircuts, their tattoos, their earrings, their smoking and drinking and their holidays, a lot of which I can't afford for myself because I'm being forced against my will by our so-called caring governments to pay for someone else's inflated life style. A lifestyle they haven't earned. Most of these poor people as you call them are poor because they choose to do nothing about their financial situation. If they're not in the pub soaking in alcohol what few brains they have left, they're stuck in front of a damn television watching the most mindless garbage imaginable. Garbage, by the way, that once again is produced against my will, with my tax money! If these so-called poor people are so concerned about their poverty, why don't they stay out of the pubs, turn off their television and study something in order to better themselves? But no, they don't do that because it's easier to vote for some disgusting left wing government who will steal my hard earned money and hand it over to them. Why should they have a lifestyle of their own choosing financed by someone else? By what principal or value can anyone claim a right to something he has not earned?'

Suzanne shrugged her shoulders in resignation.

'When you put it that way I can understand your frustration. But what else can anyone do with people who don't want to help themselves?'

'Nothing. The question is what to do with those who are unable to support themselves as opposed to those who choose not to support themselves. What do you want to do?' he asked. 'And that is the question that should be asked; what do *you* want to do? If you wish to help them, then help them. Nobody is stopping you from putting your hand in your pocket and giving whatever you want to, but if someone else doesn't want to help, what right has anyone got to force him to do so? How can we call ourselves civilised if we constantly initiate the use of force to get our own way? One man's misfortune should not give him the right to enslave another and nor should it give the government the right to steal on his behalf. Whatever you have been told in the past, the truth and absolute reality is that the philosophy of altruism is the most vile, most cancerous disease that has ever been inflicted on the human race and if it is not arrested and reversed, we will end up by entering a new Dark Ages where the law of the jungle is supreme and morality is reduced to "every man for himself". This is the true nature of altruism and the obscene policy of taxation. It is pure evil and any political party that claims love of mankind as its motivating force should have the total abolition of taxation as its long-term policy. Slavery is not an acceptable method of existence and nor can it be sustainable indefinitely. Inevitably, the situation will arise whereby there will be far too many parasites feeding off far too few producers. In fact it's not long in coming. Just look at the state of the once proud and powerful German economy as one example. No highly developed, industrialised society, like those in the Western world, can be maintained indefinitely without a rational philosophy to guide it. Without a proper, objective base for it to stand on, it will crumble and collapse and that is precisely what you are seeing now.'

'So, if taxation is abolished, where will the money come from for the government to operate, even as you say, it sticks to its morally proper functions?' asked Suzanne.

Bradshaw continued, 'You'd think that that would have been solved a long time ago. I once read of an interesting solution proposed by an extremely clever woman. She suggested the government charge a fee of say one percent on all contractual agreements in return for which, if any disagreements occurred between the contracting parties, they would have recourse to the courts. Those who choose not to pay the fee have would have no recourse to the courts. In other words, those who want this legal service provided by government, pay for it, those who don't, don't. It's called freedom of choice. When you consider the enormous sums of money, billions and billions of pounds that exchanges hands in the business world today, one percent in itself would be a huge amount. Of course it would not be limited to the world of business. To give you a simple example, every employee could voluntarily decide whether or not to pay the fee on his salary or wages. If he chose not to and his employer failed to pay him, then he would not have any recourse to the courts; he hadn't paid for the service. If on the other hand he chose to pay the fee, his claim against his employer would be settled in the courts. The same principle would apply to rental agreements, leases, mortgages, etcetera and every other form of legal commercial exchange that exists. I haven't done the sums myself, but even if the voluntary one percent fee that was suggested became two percent, it would be light years less than we are forced to pay now. Nobody would be forced to pay for any service he did not wish to use but would be free to spend the rewards of his efforts on those things that are a priority to him. With what each individual saved by not being forced to contribute to services he choose not to use, those who chose to invest in their children's' education or in health care would be free to do so. Those who chose to lend support to those they consider less fortunate would also have funds to do so. That's proper freedom, not that excuse we have for it at the moment.'

'We're always hearing about how intelligent our politicians are and how clever and highly qualified and respected our academics. Why haven't they worked out some alternative system? Are they now adding mental bankruptcy to their moral bankruptcy? The truth is they don't want to change the status quo. The academics are still absorbed with the philosophy of altruism and both they and the politicians are besotted with power. Power is their sole motive. Neither wants mankind to be free. They both lust after control of their fellow man.'

'The only way to get rid of their oppressive yoke is to denounce the academics' false philosophy for what it is, and to replace it with one that is in accord with Man's nature, and restrict the role of government to its proper function. If we fail in either of these, we will remain slaves until we finally return to the Dark Ages and total barbarism takes over. Those parents who claim to love their children more than anything in the world should reflect carefully. Altruism is not only destroying the current populace, it's not giving the children of tomorrow a fighting chance. Look at the state of today's youth. They're totally confused. Because philosophy is all but dead and what remains is no more than a poisonous concoction of altruism and mysticism, they lack any direction or guidance. They're told that there are no absolutes, nothing is right and nothing is wrong. Morals, principals, ethics are arbitrary and these are decided by their feelings or popular vote, not by any rational or objective philosophy. Whatever they feel is right at any given moment, is right, simply because they feel it. The next moment something entirely different is right because their feelings have changed. And of course what is right for them might not be right for you, and who are you to tell them they're wrong. As for being held accountable for one's actions; don't be silly. If there's no right and wrong, how can anyone be accountable? If there are no consequences for one's actions, how can a sense of responsibility develop? Punishment has become farcical in most instances; it's no more than a mild rebuke or a slight rap over the knuckles. The most absurd excuses are made for the most offensive behaviour. In the absence of any rational, guiding philosophy what else can be expected? Is it any wonder they turn to alcohol and drugs. Is it any wonder that teenage suicide is on the increase? In spite of there not being a rational philosophy, today's youth senses that something is not right and the brighter ones, not being able to conceptualise a just world, either become reclusive and introverted or turn to drugs and often end up committing suicide, whilst the not so intelligent become mere anti-social misfits.'

'When a philosophy of slavery and theft is adopted, when the guiding principle states that your sole purpose in life is to provide for anyone and everyone but yourself, it is not a quantum leap to conclude that everyone else must be here to provide for you. Don't be surprised when the crime figures soar and the violence and hooligan behaviour you read about daily in the newspapers occurs – you let it happen. You express disgust when you hear of the huge increase in the amount of violent crime, yet you willingly vote for government after government whose main method of dealing with its own citizens is force. Is this the freedom that our parents and grandparents died for in two world wars?'

'You've got me interested.' said Suzanne. 'I agree, taxation is far too high and if I accept what you have just said, how would you implement the abolition of taxation?'

'Unfortunately it would take a long time. It wouldn't be in my lifetime. It would probably take at least two generations and many other things would need to be in place before it could be fully put into effect. Firstly a rational, objective philosophy that is in accordance with Man's nature has to be formulated, disseminated, accepted and adopted by the population in general. A clear and just understanding of property rights must be included in this philosophy. The poison of any altruistic philosophy needs to be totally discredited on moral grounds and discarded, and those who choose not to discard it can be seen for the parasites and enslavers they really are. We need a proper written constitution clearly defining and restricting the role of government, together with a bill of rights to protect the country's citizens from any possible abuses by government. Once this has been achieved, most of those who currently rely on handouts from the taxpayer would have to be weaned off them. In order to prevent the possibility of any widespread social discord or misery, it would be necessary to continue these handouts to a certain sections of the population, such as old aged pensioners who are too old to work, until death relieves the taxpayer of their burden. To strip an old age pensioner of his pension may in many cases leave him totally destitute. To avoid this and to maintain general public acceptance of these changes, such pensions would have to remain in place. Medical benefits and housing subsidies would also have to be considered in a like manner to those in this age group.'

'Those of working age would have reduced "state" benefits. These reductions would be calculated on a sliding scale, dependant on age, the amount of contributions already made and the number of working years remaining. That national disgrace, more commonly known as the National Health Service, would permit no new "members" and would eventually be wound down until it no longer existed. Those people excluded from new National Health Service participation could choose to join a medical private scheme, as could anyone else who wished to. The choice would be theirs. Schools, hospitals and the like would have to be privatised and all taxpayer subsidised housing sold off. The railway system would have to be re-privatised; properly this time, and replace the abortive mess that currently exists. It must be realised that one can only rightfully expect that which one has earned. If one does not earn it, one goes without or relies on voluntary charity. It must be realised that there is no such thing as a free lunch anymore and nor will there ever be again. It must be realised and accepted that no matter how big a mob or gang that gives its support, no one will ever again have the right to enslave anyone else. Only then could any serious and meaningful reduction in taxation commence. In view of the fact that those over the age of forty would have to be provided for to some extent until death, full implementation would only come into effect in approximately fifty years time. By far the hardest task to accomplish would be the acceptance of a new philosophy based on rationally derived individual rights, not "human rights" as they are currently called, with all individuals having equal rights. If this first step could not be achieved then the process could proceed no further and this is what the supporters of altruism fully understand. Hence their frenzied attempts to justify their point of view with emotive arguments, and their total refusal to discuss their philosophy on a rational or moral basis. In open and honest debate, their false arguments would be exposed for the lies that they really are and that is why they tell us there is no right or wrong and that our feelings, not our minds, should dictate our actions. Their arguments are as hollow as their beliefs and it is only because of moral default by those who oppose them, that they have got away with their lies and falsehoods for this long. This is the eternal disgrace of all so-called conservatives and the Conservative Party. They both lack any moral conviction and thereby leave us all open to the abuses of the left wing in general and the Labour Party in particular. And what makes it worse is they know of a system that once almost existed, that allowed Man to live as freely as his nature intended; it was called Capitalism, but they didn't then and they don't now, have the moral courage to defend it.'

'As I've already mentioned, in most democratic countries, there is constitutional provision that expressly prohibits involuntary servitude. If Man's basic means of survival is to work in order to support himself, then by taking any part of his remuneration, against his will or by the use of force, for any reason whatsoever, must surely constitute involuntary servitude. Taxation is a form of involuntary servitude. Any country that practices force against its own citizens cannot claim to be just and therefore cannot claim to be civilised. Why have we let this disastrous situation come about? There are three basic causes, the lust of power for power's sake by politicians, the philosophy of altruism perpetuated by the academics, and the acceptance of these two insults by what can only be described as willing slaves.'

'Firstly, whilst it is illegal for a private individual to use force against another, as in the case of a criminal, it is not illegal for government to do so. I ask you to consider the expression: "*when such and such a political party* ***comes into power***". This is an absurd notion, but one that has gone unchallenged for far too long. It is true that government is entrusted with certain powers to act on the peoples' behalf, but that does not mean it has an open-ended mandate to do as it wishes and it certainly does not give it the right to enslave anyone, for any reason whatsoever.'

'Every government minister, even the Prime Minister, is a public servant. Servants do not come into power; they enter servitude. There are far too many of these public servants who believe they can wield unlimited power over the general populace without any restraint of any kind. Far too many of them believe that they are some type of superior being, destined to rule by decree over the rest of mankind. In a democracy, public servants are there to carry out the wishes of the people; the people are **not** there to carry out the wishes of the public servants.' 'This does not mean however that the majority can possess the right to enslave the minority in order to avoid the necessity of providing for themselves. The last fifty years has seen the democratic system throughout the entire world become nothing more than a synonym for mob rule. He with the biggest gang cracks the whip. There are those in this country who think it is unnecessary to have a written constitution. I submit that for this reason alone, it is vitally necessary. And equally essential is a Bill of Rights, in order to protect each and every individual from abuse from his own government.'

'The second reason is the practice of altruism. Altruism is the immoral philosophy that effectively reduces Man's sole purpose in life to that of a slave, a slave for the benefit of all others but not his own. It states that the welfare of others should be his only concern, and any thought of his own happiness is the ultimate sin. This is the openly proclaimed philosophy of the Left; it is the modus operandi of the parasite. It is the belief that a man does not have to earn his rewards in life, that he is entitled to them merely because he exists. The practical implementation of altruism in this country has been socialism and the discriminatory taxation associated with it. The welfare state was introduced after the Second World War by that never-to-be-forgiven Attlee Labour government. They are in large responsible for that disgusting condition in which we now all exist. The welfare state necessitates that the welfare of one man be at the expense of another. The Left's answer to every problem, real or otherwise, requires a victim. The last fifty years have been nothing more than an endless altruistic relay, with one government passing the Socialist baton to the next, save Mrs Thatcher, who dropped it momentarily. This is the morality and true nature of altruism. A man's life is his own. It is sacred. It is not to be disposed of by any other party, whether that other party be an individual, a gang of thugs or an elected government, regardless of reason, cause or for whose benefit. One man's misfortune cannot give him the right to enslave another. The ends do not justify the means. The only proper way to deal with such unfortunate cases is by voluntary charity. Whatever you think the function of government should be, it cannot be to steal from one man that which he has earned, to give to another who has not earned.'

'Freedom is by far the most potent enemy against poverty and at the end of the day the only moral and only practical way to overcome poverty. The freest countries have always been the richest, with any citizen taking part in the general economy enjoying a standard of living far higher than his counterpart in less free countries. Apart from the moral aspect, altruism doesn't alleviate the problem in practice; it never has done and it never will. It is increasingly obvious that the larger the public trough, the more snouts it attracts. Let's briefly look at what altruism and the welfare state have achieved in reality? They've achieved the welfare of no one. Have you ever heard of the brain drain of the sixties and seventies? The eighties and nineties aren't mentioned to the same extent – there aren't as many brains as before to drain. The best of this country's brains were driven from these shores to greener pastures, through punitive taxation or lack of research and development resources due to nationalisation by socialistic governments. Do you remember when taxation at the top end was nineteen and sixpence in the pound? Ninety five percent stolen from the most able and dished out to any parasite with a begging bowl. Their only sin was to have brains, ambition and the capacity for hard work. Most of these people never returned. Not only did the country lose them, but they also lost their offspring. Entire families of highly intelligent individuals were gone forever. The best breeding stock sent packing so that the lazy and the unambitious could enjoy a lifestyle far beyond the capacity of their own abilities. This is the true nature of altruism. And all this is done in the name of love of mankind! The contribution of such people had they remained in this country, could have and would have resulted in a better standard of living for all who participated in the general economy, without suffering the evils of altruism. The proof of this statement lies in the fact that the countries to where these people fled, all enjoy a better standard of living than we do here. And after over half a century of this vile system the poor are still with us! Nothing has changed. The whole disgusting experiment has been a complete and utter failure. But do we learn? No, we just keep on voting for more of the same poison that's slowly killing us. Was nothing learned from the former Soviet Union? The Soviet state collapsed because it was financially ruined. It was broke. It couldn't continue any longer. So what do the voters in this country do? They don't vote for the poison labelled Communism, they in their wisdom, vote for the poison labelled Socialism and thereby choose an even more drawn-out death; and that death will come. And those of us who don't want to drink from this contaminated well have our heads shoved down it and are forced to drink until we drown. What is Man without his freedom? Those who proclaim their love of mankind, what have they achieved? And as for the left wing liberals who proclaim that the ego is evil; what have they achieved by their attempted destruction of "self"? A generation of aimless souls who have no self-discipline, no self-control, no self-reliance, no self-confidence, no self-esteem and worst of all, no self-respect. And once Man loses his self-respect, he has no respect for anyone else or anyone else's property. This is what the philosophy of selflessness achieves – the opposite of what was intended. A society of drunkards or dysfunctional drug addicts, all running from reality and chasing any and all forms of escapism available because the reality they have created is too hideous to bear.'

'And finally, and arguably most disgusting of all, we have the absurd situation whereby the productive slaves offer no resistance to their enslavement. Trained like Pavlov's dogs, they willing accept their fate, occasionally muttering amongst themselves, "There's nothing we can do about it". These modern day slaves offer no resistance. They merely accept their lot in life, grateful for any morsel not stolen by their governments, then unaided put on their shackles and pick up the task masters whip. Perhaps such a spineless, insipid lot deserve no better. The odd person who actively resists is imprisoned for tax evasion; for trying to protect his own hard earned money he is put in prison and branded a common criminal. It is a moral obscenity that a man be penalised for his enterprise.'

'Now you know why I'm so strongly opposed to taxation. Obsessed as you put it.' Suzanne was silent for a moment before she said,
'My father would have liked you James.'

Nightfall approached and complete darkness enveloped the cottage by the time they had finished painting. Bradshaw had started the log fire earlier in the afternoon and now pleasant warmth spread throughout the small cottage. He completed the final stroke with the roller and placed it in the tray. He stretched his back and then looked at his watch. It was gone eight o'clock
'We'd better be going or else you'll have to pay me double time.' he said jokingly.
'I thought we'd go that restaurant we went to before, and then spend the night here.' replied Suzanne. She wasn't joking.

~ Chapter 8 ~

Summer turned into autumn and autumn into winter. The days grew shorter and the nights longer and colder and Bradshaw didn't look forward to his weekly trips with the same relish he had during the long, warm summer. The countryside in both England and France had turned from a lush green to the browns of autumn and then to the greys of winter. Over the previous few months, Suzanne had accompanied Bradshaw to France on two or three occasions. She neither hid nor advertised the fact. It had been the cause of several heated exchanges between herself and her brother.

'What the hell do you think you're doing hanging around with a van driver?' he shouted at her one morning

'A van unloader.' she corrected him.

'You're far too good for the likes of him.' he fumed, ignoring her sarcasm.

'I wish I was.' she replied simply.

'This nonsense stops now. I forbid you to see him again. If you do, I'll fire him on the spot. You're the laughing stock of all the drivers.'
'I don't care for anyone else's opinion. Mine is the only one that counts. I don't seek anyone's approval. I'll see him as often as I want. You might own sixty percent of this company and therefore you can fire him, but if you do, you'll buy out my forty percent immediately and I'll never set foot in this place again.'
'You can't threaten me like that. You know I can't afford to buy you out.'
'Well then, you'll keep your nose out of my business and you'll leave Bradshaw alone, do you understand me? Life's about making choices and I've made mine, now you'll have to make yours.' Paul Crookes had stormed from the office, slamming the door behind him.

They were returning from one of their trips together one chilly evening when they were stopped at customs. The customs official was a thin insipid looking, pasty-faced man. His manner was officious and abrupt. He typified that type of bureaucrat who, endowed with a small amount of power, meant to use it to the full limit. He was a petty little man. He ordered Bradshaw to pull his van over near a small brick building that served as the customs office. The pasty-faced man was obviously in charge. He ordered two of his underlings to unload the van and they robotically obeyed without question. When they had completed their task, one of the underlings went into the office and returned with Pasty-Face. He looked at Bradshaw with an expression that was little less than distain.

'So this is for personal use only is it?' he asked with a sneer.
'That's right.' replied Bradshaw, looking Pasty-Face straight in the eye.
'I don't believe you.' snapped Pasty-Face.
'Believe what you want.' said Bradshaw.
'Don't get smart with me. I'm in charge around here.' The customs official's face was beginning to redden. 'When did you last buy for personal use?' he demanded, with more than a touch of sarcasm on the words "personal use".
'Why ask me?' replied Bradshaw, 'You've just told me you don't believe me, so why ask me any more questions?'
'Right.' screamed Pasty-Face. He was losing face in front of his two underlings who were standing idly by, not knowing what to say or do. 'Right, I'm confiscating all of this.' he said, waving his finger in the general direction of Bradshaw's stockpile. 'And as for you, I'm charging you for importing alcohol and cigarettes for non-personal use and attempting to evade the tax thereon. Follow me to the office.'

After he had been charged, Bradshaw was allowed to go. He and Suzanne drove out of Portsmouth in silence. Finally Suzanne spoke.
'I'll speak to Terry Adams first thing on Monday morning. He's our company solicitor.'
'I don't want a solicitor.' replied Bradshaw bluntly. 'This is a moral issue, not a legal one. I'll conduct my own defence. I know what a solicitor will do, apart from charging me a fortune. He'll want me to plead guilty and then he'll go to great lengths to tell the court that this my first offence and that I'm normally a good citizen, that I'm repentant

and have shown remorse, that it won't happen again and that I deserve a second chance and suggest I be sentenced to community service, which in itself is just another form of slavery. Well, I'm not repentant. This isn't my first offence, it's just the first time I've been caught and it probably won't be the last.'

'You won't win James.'

'Of course I won't. The state will see to that. But I'll never win if I capitulate to their immoral laws either.'

The trial date was set for two months time. Suzanne finally convinced Bradshaw not to make any more trips to France.

'They'll be on the lookout for you and you'll only make matters worse.'

'All right, I won't go again until all this is over.' he said begrudgingly. 'I can spend the time preparing my defence.'

~ CHAPTER 9 ~

Somehow word got out about Bradshaw's arrest. Paul Crookes was delighted when he found out. He stalked into his sister's office without knocking and in his loud raucous voice demanded that Bradshaw be fired immediately.

'We don't employ criminals. That's one of your rules remember.'

'I remember,' she replied quietly, 'but to my knowledge Bradshaw hasn't been found guilty of anything as yet.'

'I don't give a damn. I want him out of here right now.'

'Fine.' she said. 'Just give me a few minutes to clear out my desk, because if he goes, so do I.' Paul Crookes stormed from her office shouting a string of obscenities.

'So?' said Benny slyly as they were driving along the motorway, 'what happened to Mr High-and-Mighty? I thought you don't do anything dishonest.'

'I don't.' answered Bradshaw evenly.
'That's not what I heard. I told you everyone's got a fiddle goin'. You're no different from anyone else.'
'Shut up Benny, you have no idea what you're talking about.'

~ Chapter 10~

The trial began on a crisp January morning. Bradshaw took his place in the courtroom. The prosecutor dressed in his wig and gown and his assistant sat at a table not far away. The judge entered and they all rose, and when he was seated, they all followed suit. Bradshaw had entered a plea of not guilty. The proceedings started with the prosecution calling Mr Pasty-Face, the customs official as its first witness. He described how he had, on that night in December, made a series of spot checks on vehicles disembarking from France. The defendant, he said, was driving one of the vehicles he inspected. He identified Bradshaw as the driver. He told the court that the official customs records showed that the defendant had been making almost weekly trips to France for the past several months. They had secretly monitored and recorded his trips and Pasty-Face rattled off a list of dates and times. On each occasion Bradshaw's van had been full of alcohol and cigarettes and the sheer volume precluded that it was all for personal use. He regarded Bradshaw with a look of distain. Bradshaw declined to cross-examine. Pasty-Face's two underlings were called and questioned by the prosecution. They corroborated the evidence Pasty-Face had already given, but with less enthusiasm. Again Bradshaw declined to cross-examine. With an air of smug superiority, the prosecution concluded its case. The judge announced that after a short break the court would hear the case for the defence.

When he re-entered the court, Bradshaw did not notice that Suzanne Crookes was seated in the gallery.
'Are you ready Mr Bradshaw?' asked the judge.
'I am Your Honour. The defence does not wish to call any witnesses, it only wishes to read a statement to the court.'
The judge imperceptibly raised his eyebrows.
'All right Mr Bradshaw. Proceed, but try to make it brief and keep it to the point.' There was a slight hint of exasperation in his voice.
'I stand here accused of importing alcohol and tobacco for uses other than personal and evading taxation on these goods. I would like to deal with the later charge as I do not intend to defend the former.' he began. 'The defence contends that the case before the court is not a legal issue, but a moral one. In a country that considers itself to be civilised, the only proper relationship between two or more parties, can only be one that is voluntary and to mutual benefit. Any other form of relationship must be one that is coercive or based on the outright use of force. These later types of relationships can in no way be described as moral, and therefore not proper in a civilised country. Clearly

the issue of taxation falls into the later type. For a man to have any part of the product of his labour, no matter how small, taken from him against his will, by the use of force, can in no-way be considered either voluntary or to mutual benefit. And yet this precisely how the taxation system operates. Taxation, by any honest definition, is legalised theft, and any man who does not give his consent to be robbed, is subjected to the only other means of collection; force. In other words, taxation itself is immoral. It contravenes every accepted norm of civilised behaviour. The kindest description of the taxation system would be to call it involuntary servitude, which is just another term for slavery; it turns every honest, hardworking man into a sacrificial animal; into a slave of the state. A free man by definition is neither a sacrificial animal nor a slave and is not to be treated as such, and since I do not regard myself as either a sacrificial animal or a slave, I will no longer allow anyone, for whatever reason, to treat me as one. This evil form of slavery must be opposed at every opportunity, fought and defeated at all costs if Man is to be free and live as Man's fundamental nature dictates he should live.'

'In any hierarchy of rights, all sides of the political spectrum agree that Man's right to life takes precedence over all others – without life, all and any other rights are impossible. Surely it follows that Man's right to support his life becomes his second most important right. If not, the "right to life" becomes meaningless. Man's basic means of survival is to work in order to support himself. By taking any part of the product of his labour, for any reason whatsoever, against his will, can only be seen as a threat to his right to his own life.'

'In most civilised countries, there are provisions in their constitutions that expressly prohibit involuntary servitude. Why does this not include taxation? Why is the government above its own laws? This type of abuse is typical of dictatorships, not of democracies. It is not the type of action that any country that calls itself civilised should sanction.'

'Taxation also totally ignores another established and fully accepted law – the law concerning the relationship between principal and agent. The purpose of government is to act as an agent to protect the individual rights of its citizens. Let me be perfectly clear on this matter. An individual cannot, under the laws of this country, allocate to someone else acting as his agent, a right that he himself does not possess. Surely it follows that when a government is appointed as the agent of the people, that government cannot possess rights that do not apply to its principal, that is to its individual citizens. It is patently obvious that if the principal does not have the right to steal or to enslave, then neither can his agent. The only objective, rational and moral conclusion one can draw from any honest interpretation of this law is that the government is also legally prohibited from theft. Since taxation is no more than a form of theft, no government can make it legal by merely passing laws. And this is not altered by the number of voters who think it does. No number of individuals no matter how much of a majority they may represent, can vote others in to slavery or "legalise" theft by government decree. This is the modus operandi of thugs, of gangsters, of dictators, it is the modus operandi of this government, it is the modus operandi of all governments.'

'Yet another accepted norm is ignored when the issue of taxation is concerned and that accepted norm is the widely held belief that the end does not justify the means. It is obvious therefore that all those who condone taxation believe that the end does justify the means. In reality, that translates to "anything goes, as long as I think it's right".' The only logical conclusion of that befuddled belief is that if a man is denied that which he has earned, then it is inevitable that he will pursue that which he has not earned. In other words, if he does not have an absolute right to the product of his labour, then he will have no choice but to expropriate the efforts of others by any means available. And who will be able to blame him? Definitely not those who believe that the end justifies the means. These individuals would be acting no differently than the government already does. I would think that is patently obvious that the belief that the end justifies the means is an open invitation to anarchy. Let the government not be surprised when more and more disaffected people follow the government's own example and your courtrooms become overcrowded with people just like me.'

'Taxation has become a tool used by politicians to buy votes and redistribute wealth, with the producers in the economy being forced to pay for the parasites. Do you ever hear a politician of any ilk talk about a redistribution of effort or productivity? It also results in the fact that any individual who pays tax, being forced into the position of financing a political party whose views and policies might be diametrically opposed to his own. I don't believe that I would be considered unfair to describe this vile practice as a breach of the right to freedom of speech. In so much as no reasonable man would expect a Jewish person to be forced to subscribe to a pro Nazi publication, no more would a reasonable man find it acceptable for a man who believes in freedom to be forced to subscribe to the activities of a statist government. If a government's only means of raising money is by theft and slavery, it is clearly evident that they are as mentally inept as they are morally bankrupt and do not deserve to govern anyone. And to anyone who claims that this is the meaning and result of living in a democracy, I say democracy has become nothing more than a synonym for mob rule. He with the biggest gang cracks the whip. I work for my own benefit, not the benefit of others, and I will not apologise for it. With all due respect Your Honour, any and all remuneration I receive in return from my labour is mine by right. Not because I have stolen it, not because I have enslaved another, not because I have extracted it by coercion or by force, but because I have **earned** it. I did not deprive the government of any of its money; it was never the government's money in the first place; all I attempted to do was prevent the government from stealing mine. Mine by right, mine because I earned it.'

'I have saved the most compelling argument for last Your Honour. Man's nature requires that he be free. It is the very essence of his being. Man's nature does not permit him to live qua Man in any other way. He is not designed to live under the yoke of slavery; his nature will not permit it. In this regard Man has no choice, it is the way he his, it is his nature. History, from time immemorial, is a succession of liberation struggles, battles for freedom, and endless fights against oppression. Just look at the history of this country. The loss of the American colonies was due directly to the imposition of an immoral tax. Many of the grievances in India sixty years ago resulted from unfair taxation practice. The nineteen sixties in this country saw the greatest loss every recorded of well educated, talented, gifted people, fleeing this country en masse as a direct result of punitive taxation. You will probably remember it as the brain drain. In most cases these people and their offspring were lost to this country forever. Their skills were eagerly accepted in their new countries; they were not punished for being ambitious, for being talented. They were rewarded and appreciated. They were not forced to forgo basic essentials they needed in order to provide luxuries for the lazy and unambitious as they were, and I am, in this country.'

'Against my will, I am forced to provide childcare for the young children of others but deprived from putting a roof over my own head and saving for my old age.'

'Against my will, when these children grow older, I am forced to provide for their education, but deprived from putting a roof over my own head and saving for my old age.'

'Against my will, when these children become young adults, I am forced to pay for them to attend university but deprived from putting a roof over my own head and saving for my old age. If they are not prepared to finance their own futures, on what basis should I?'

'Against my will, I am forced to provide taxi fares and private tuition for convicted drug pushers, but deprived from putting a roof over my own head and saving for my old age.'

'Against my will, I am forced to provide cigarettes, alcohol, tattoos, designer clothes, and designer hairstyles for anyone who has decided working for a living is not for him, but deprived from putting a roof over my own head and saving for my old age.'

'Against my will, I am forced to provide juvenile delinquents with all expenses paid holidays to the Caribbean so they can "get in touch with their roots", but deprived from putting a roof over my own head and saving for my old age.'

'Against my will, I am forced to provide housing for any unemployed, dysfunctional misfit who wishes to breed without any restraint, but deprived from putting a roof over my own head and saving for my old age.'

'Against my will, I am forced to constantly fill that bottomless pit known as the "Third World", but deprived from putting a roof over my own head and saving for my old age.'

'Against my will, I am forced to pay for countless "public services" which I never, ever use, but deprived from putting a roof over my own head and saving for my old age.'

'The list is endless. Are you getting the message? I am forced to have no life and no future in order to provide for those are too lazy to do so for themselves and I am not going to allow anyone to treat me in this manner ever again. When Man is stripped of all hope, only desperation remains. With all due respect Your Honour, your society is on a collision course with reality.'

'Thousands of British men and women lost their lives in two world wars, fighting for freedom and liberty. They did not fight and die only to see successive governments turn us into slaves. They fought for freedom, because Man, by his nature, has to be free. In any country that considers itself civilised, no one can have the right to steal, especially the government, whose only moral purpose is to protect the rights of its citizens, not abuse those rights.'

'If I am found guilty, you not only condemn me, you condemn yourselves, your children and you children's children to a lifetime of slavery; if you find me not guilty, you set us all free. The choice between a civilised future and one of barbaric slavery lies in your hands, and your choice will reflect your moral status and your true concern with, and love of, mankind.'

'Taxation is evil. Not only does it make slaves of all decent men, but over time it also teaches men that slavery is their normal state, not to be questioned and definitely not to be opposed. The proof of this lies in the fact that I stand here today, accused in a court of law. In other words slavery is not only sanctioned by custom, it is also sanctioned by law.'

'Finally I stand here before you today, not because of any immoral act I have committed. I stand here because I refuse to be a slave and remain silent. I stand here because I refuse to be stolen from and remain silent. I stand here because I wish to be free and will not remain silent until I am. I stand here because my nature demands it. My life belongs to me; it does not belong to the state, nor does it belong to anyone else, regardless of how "noble" their cause may be. And remember, unless all men are free, no man is free. The defence rests Your Honour.'

A hushed quiet fell over the courtroom. Even the judge remained silent. People looked at one another, saying nothing. At last the silence was broken by the sharp sound of a solitary pair of hands clapping clearly in the public gallery. It was only then that Bradshaw looked up and saw Suzanne Crookes. He smiled and put two fingers to his forehead in salute. Others joined in the applause. The judge, not bothering to call for order, left the courtroom.

~ Chapter 11~

Darkness had come some hours before and along with it a nasty chill. The old man put down his book and turned off the bedside light. He pulled the blankets close and move closer to the woman sleeping next to him.

'Good night Suzanne.' he whispered softly. 'Thanks for everything.' During the night the old man breathed his last breathe. James Bradshaw was free at last.

Printed in the United States
87102LV00005B/31-45/A

9 781425 966140